SOLID GROUND

*Coffee Shop Chronicles to Anchor Your
Heart and Soul*

Jan Unfried

Cover photograph: Sunset at Morro Rock by Jerry Unfried

Follow Common Ground and Solid Ground on Facebook @ commongroundchronicles

Jan Unfried
Visit my website at www.janunfried.com

Printed in the United States of America

First Printing: October 2019
J & J Unfried Publishing

ISBN- 978-1-6969-4249-2

Books and Resources by Jan Unfried

Coffee Shop Chronicles Series:

1) *Common Ground, Coffee Shop Chronicles to Warm Your Heart and Soul*

2) *Solid Ground, Coffee Shop Chronicles to Anchor Your Heart and Soul*

3) *Higher Ground, Coffee Shop Chronicles to Lift Your Heart and Soul* (coming Fall of 2020)

Jan's Blog: https://www.janunfried.com/blog

Endorsements

Once again, God has used Jan to capture the power of His story unfolding in the lives of others who live life in organic spaces for Jesus. If you have ever thought your story is insignificant or does not have the power to change lives or move the heart of someone in need, then grab a cup of coffee and allow the Lord to reveal his desire to change the trajectory of people's history through simple obedience and faith illustrated in this book. These stories will inspire, ignite, and encourage you to courageously live a life devoted to Jesus on Solid Ground.

-Darren Reed, Lead Pastor
Olive Knolls Nazarene Church

In the heart of every follower of Jesus is a deep desire to share our faith in natural ways. I call this Organic Outreach. One of the best ways to get fired up, inspired, and equipped to share our faith is to hear stories of God's redemptive power. When we hear testimonies from people who are shining the light of Jesus, we want to get in the game and be a part of God's work in this world. I pray that this collection of stories will inspire your heart, ignite your passion, and open your mouth to share the amazing Good News of Jesus with the people you encounter each day.

-Rev. Dr. Kevin G. Harney
Co-Founder of Organic Outreach
International (organicoutreach.org)
Lead Pastor of Shoreline Church in
Monterey, Ca.

Over the many years we have personally known Jan, she has developed a well-deserved reputation as a faithful follower of Christ in the minds and hearts of us and all who know her. It's no surprise that this retired teacher has been drawn to stories in which we could see God's hand at work among us, and we pray that these stories are a source of encouragement to you as well.

–Rob and Debie Songer
District Superintendent and Pastors
Central California District
Church of the Nazarene

Those who read Jan's thoughtful compilation of God-stories will hear credible witnesses tell of God's unmistakable current day activity. Followers of Jesus will be drawn to greater faith in and love for Jesus. Non-followers will be drawn to consider, or reconsider, responding and relating to the living God Who cares, Who knows, Who speaks and Who acts today.

–Hal and Debbi Perkins
Authors of Discipled by Jesus, If Jesus Were a
Parent, and 4 other books on discipling
Partnering with Dan Bohi Ministries to
strengthen others in growing as and
making   Christlike   disciples.

Acknowledgements

Writing *Solid Ground* has been so rewarding! There were so many people willing to share their stories! Outstanding thanks to all of you! Your testimonies of God's goodness and power strengthened my faith. I know the same will happen as others read your accounts. There would not be a *Coffee Shop Chronicles* 2 without you.

Thank you to my husband, Jerry, for giving me feedback, letting me drag you all over the place to share my book with others, and for being the best possible husband for me! You help hone my skills and keep me on my toes! We are definitely in this adventure together!

Patti King, my friend and editor, thank you for dropping everything to read and edit my stories. You have been a great support and encouragement to me through my book projects. I am blessed to have you in my life!

I am so grateful to Jesus Christ, my Lord and Savior. You are my Rock and the Solid Ground on which I stand. All other ground is "sinking sand." You are the Author and Finisher of my faith, and I have counted on You all along the way to help me complete my second book.

Table of Contents

INTRODUCTION

Common Ground, my first book in the *Coffee Shop Chronicles* series, was all about coffee. It told of the ins and outs of coffee, and the majority of stories centered on meetings in a coffee shop or over a cup of coffee. *Solid Ground* stories are not about coffee, per se, but they are coffee-shop worthy, and they truly will anchor your heart and soul into the *Solid Ground* of Jesus Christ. Another reason why the second book in the series connects to coffee was made evident during a recent coffee farm tour in Hawaii. There were many correlations between the coffee bean's journey and the journey of those who shared their accounts.

While visiting the Big Island, we decided to tour the Greenwell Coffee Farm. Bronson, our tour guide, was the grandson of a small coffee farmer in Kona, Hawaii. He grew up working the soil, harvesting the coffee berries, and helping process the beans. His rich experience made him the perfect guide. He explained how coffee seeds are carefully planted and cultivated in just the right soil and temperature. The coffee trees are pruned to maintain a height that will bear the weight of the fruit without bending or breaking the branches. Complimentary vegetation is planted around the coffee trees to provide proper shading and protection from damaging winds and elements of nature.

The best coffee comes from the "cherries" that are picked by hand. Farm workers only choose the fruit with a bright red hue that shows they are ripe for harvest. The coffee bean is surrounded by layers of pulp, parchment skin, and slick cellular tissue. These layers are carefully removed, and the coffee beans must then be sun-dried to prepare them for storage. They are spread out on drying tables where they are turned regularly and covered at night or when a tropical rain passes overhead.

Once the beans are sorted for size, weight, and imperfections, the "green coffee" is bagged and ready for roasting. The roasting process is conducted with carefully-controlled temperatures and duration. At just the right degree of heat, a fragrant oil locked inside the beans begins to emerge. At this point of the roasting progression, the flavor and aroma of the coffee we drink is produced.

As you read these pages, think of each story and life in terms of the coffee seed. God "plants" us in just the right spot. He places the right people and circumstances around us to help prepare us for harvesting. When we give our lives to the Lordship of Jesus, we begin abiding in Jesus, the true vine. The Father prunes our branches so that we can bear fruit. We also must allow Him to begin removing the surplus layers. Our sin, dysfunction, childhood experiences (both good and bad), and belief systems (both true and erroneous) are stripped away to expose the healthy and whole "bean" we were intended to be. The truth of God's Word and the fact that He is willing to bear our unneeded baggage is liberating. It sometimes takes a while for us to fully realize the benefits of His mercy and grace, but He is patient with us during the process.

An additional fact that we learned at the coffee farm is that the "unwanted" pulp is actually used to make antioxidant-rich beverages, or it is fermented to create a powerful fertilizer that is placed back into the soil of the newly developing plants. Likewise, God uses the dross of our lives to enrich the lives of others. As they hear of God's redeeming work and see the results of His life-giving purpose, they are encouraged in their own growth.

Then God starts His refining work in us! We learn to trust God as the heat and duration of our trials continue to develop us into the person God wants us to be. He unlocks the fragrance of His love as we learn to live with joy and peace no matter what our circumstances. We begin to understand what it means to enjoy fullness of life. You will be reading about people who have been through this process. Their stories will fill you with God's sweet aroma and encourage you in your faith, if you let them.

Our pastor preached a summer series through the book of John on the miraculous signs and wonders of Jesus. As we studied some of Jesus's miracles, we were challenged to examine our faith responses to these extraordinary stories. Would we just pat the Bible knowingly and feel like we had heard a good tale? Or would our faith grow as we sought the reality of Jesus at work in our own lives?

It struck me as I listened to the sermons that the same challenge was appropriate for *Solid Ground.* I had heard some amazing testimonies, and I was attempting to bring them some sense of justice as I retold them in my book. Was I just enjoying these as God's goodness in someone else's life, or was I allowing the accounts of God's restoration, healing, and power to move me closer to God and stronger in my own faith?

I have heard discussions both in and out of church circles that the miracles Jesus did in the New Testament times are not as prevalent today. The argument goes that if we just had signs like we read about in the Bible it would be so much easier to believe in the Son of God. *Solid Ground* dispels this thought. As I have written the stories of these modern-era miracles, it is evident that God **is** still at work today. We will always seek signs and wonders, but what we do with them is the key.

The testimonies that follow, like the miracles in the Bible, have some things in common. There was a great need. God's promises were claimed. Many times fellow believers supported, mentored, and interceded for the one experiencing loss, pain, or illness. However, the MAIN thing both the Biblical and the current accounts have in common is that Jesus is the answer. He is the solid rock, the firm foundation, the cornerstone, on which each person can stand. My prayer as you read these chronicles is that you will not just enjoy the stories, pat the book lovingly, and experience a warm and fuzzy feeling. My hope is that you will take the next step of faith for your own life. Dig into God's word, find the treasures He has in store for you, and get to know the Miracle Worker in a new and personal way. Let Him anchor your heart and soul in the *Solid Ground* of a deep and meaningful relationship with Him.

FOR YOUR INFORMATION:

There are some things set up in each chapter of this book to help you get the most out of *Solid Ground, Coffee Shop Chronicles to Anchor Your Heart and Soul*. Of course, you can read each chapter as a read through only. If you want to go deeper and/or use it as a daily devotional, each chapter is summarized in a section called "Soil-Sifting Summary." There are verses that support these key points in a segment called "Digging into God's Word." You are also given an opportunity to journal your thoughts about the chapter content, summary points, or scriptures on a page called "Extracting Truths and Treasures." However you chose to go through the book, I pray that your faith will be anchored more securely in the Rock!

Finally, you will find that many of the chronicles make reference to Olive Knolls Church. Olive Knolls Church of the Nazarene is in Bakersfield, California. It is my home church, and, though not exclusively, I have interviewed a lot of people from my church family. The lead pastor is Rev. Darren Reed. Rather than explaining this in each separate chapter, the church may be referred to interchangeably as Olive Knolls, Olive Knolls Church, or Olive Knolls Nazarene Church. Occasionally I will refer to the pastor as Pastor Darren. I know you all have a church body that has amazing stories like the ones you will read here. I urge you to take a friend or two to coffee and share your miracles with each other. I pray you will be encouraged and uplifted.

Christ,
Our Refuge and
Fortress

Chapter 1
OUR NAVIGATIONAL AIDE

Since you are my rock and my fortress, for the sake of your name
lead and guide me. Psalm 31:3

When you read through the Old and New Testaments, there are multiple references to God as our Rock. Songs have been written and sung through the ages declaring faith in God, our Rock. He is the One we can count on to be strong and secure, constant and dependable. There are beloved hymns like "Rock of Ages" and "The Solid Rock." We sing contemporary choruses like "Cornerstone" by Hillsong, proclaiming, "Christ alone, Cornerstone, weak made strong in the Savior's love. Through the storm, He is Lord, Lord of all." In the song "Only King Forever" by Elevation Worship, the lyrics affirm, "Our God, a firm foundation. Our rock, the only **solid ground**..."

The Psalms give us insight into the True Rock. They speak of God as our shelter, our refuge, and our defense. He is a dwelling place, a shade from the heat, and a summit of rest. God is compared to mountains which stand in grandeur—immovable, everlasting and strong. Jesus speaks of building our foundation on His words. In Peter's letter to the Christians scattered throughout Asia Minor, he refers to Jesus as the Living Stone, our Cornerstone. The list goes on as we learn that just as God provided water for the Israelites from a rock in the wilderness, He is also our source of spiritual refreshment. In 1 Samuel, Hannah rejoices in the Lord as she prays, "There is no one holy like the Lord; there is no one besides you; there is no Rock like our God" (1 Samuel 2:2).

There is an iconic rock on the Pacific coast that illustrates some of these mainstays of God's character. It is one of the most visible landmarks on the central California Coast—by land, by sea, or by air. This rock, known as Morro Rock, is in Morro Bay, California. Morro Rock is a volcanic plug which looms 576 feet at the entrance to the Morro Bay Harbor. It is part of a chain of similar inland formations, called Nine Sisters, which range from Morro Bay to San Luis Obispo.

Morro, meaning domed rock or "turban," was formed from the plug of a long-extinct volcano. Once completely surrounded by water, the Rock, also known as "The Gibraltar of the Pacific," is now connected to the mainland by a causeway that was formed using material quarried from the rock's surface. A breakwater was also formed using the extracted stone, providing protection for the harbor from strong and potentially destructive currents, tides, and waves.[1]

There are several analogies between God our Rock and Morro Rock. Just as Morro Rock provides protection and a safe haven for the once endangered Peregrine Falcons, God our Rock is our Shelter and our Dwelling Place. The rock jetties created from Morro Rock shield the harbor from pounding waves and erosion. In much the same way, we are protected from the storms of life when we trust in God. As hikers rest in the shadow that is cast by this rock of grandeur in the Pacific, we can hide and rest in the shade and the shadow of the Almighty Rock.

Some of the parallels don't quite work. God, as our Rock, is immovable, everlasting, strong, and abiding. He is unchanging;

---

[1] *Morro Rock Beach.* (n.d.). morro-bay.ca.us/383/Morro-Rock-Beach

there is no God like our God. Conversely, even though Morro Rock has been around a long time, it has changed gradually with time, weather, and man's modernization. At some point the Earth could shift and Morro Rock could be moved or even destroyed. That's why Jesus taught in Matthew 7 that we must build our lives on the foundation of His Word. It's not just about hearing His words, but it's about practicing them! When we observe God's precepts we will not experience shifting sand that doesn't support us when the waves and storms of life come our way. We will remain sure-footed. Our house will stand. The foundation will remain rock solid!

A final and particularly important comparison of God, our Rock, and Morro Rock, is their ability to lead and guide us. Mariners used Morro Rock as a navigational aid. It was so grand and unmistakable, the sight of this landmark would instantly give the seafarers their bearings. Though this physical rock is sometimes shrouded in fog, our God is never hidden from us. If we seek Him, He will reveal Himself to us. When we look to God, He is our constant and perfect Navigational Aide. He keeps us steady and on course. If we lose our way or are uncertain of the direction to head, God will lead and guide us in the right path. He is the landmark by which we should chart our life's journey.

Morgan (Burnard) Bonn has counted on God's navigation through the past couple of years. When we left her in *Common Ground* ("Your Heart's Desire" chapter), she was running a mobile coffee business and getting ready to get married. In the past couple of years, there have been a few strong waves threatening to erode her dreams and sweep her away in the undertow.

Morgan and her husband decided the best place to live would be Valencia, California. It was located midway between both their jobs.

Carter would drive to Hollywood each day, and Morgan would travel to Bakersfield to continue running her coffee company, Cloud 9. At one point they had contemplated moving the mobile unit to Valencia. Things seemed like they might be lining up, but Morgan had noticed a few cracks developing in the trailer. She decided to have the issues checked out and repaired before attempting to transport the unit to her new residence over the Grape Vine, a steep five-and-a-half mile grade at the northern end of the Tejon Pass on California's I-5.

The technician who looked at the Cloud 9 trailer knew immediately that the integrity of the unit was compromised. He kept it for two weeks to thoroughly investigate the problems. The news was not good. Apparently, according to Morgan, she had been sold a bill of goods. Though the person who originally retrofitted the trailer, converting it into a mobile coffee shop, had done a beautiful job on the surface, he had failed to reveal the precarious shape it was in. Upon opening the aluminum walls to get a better glimpse at what was going on, the new mechanic was appalled. He later told Morgan that the structure holding the trailer up was basically dry rot. He wasn't even sure how it had been holding everything together. The roof was in danger of collapsing, the walls were bowing, and he was amazed it was still intact. The weight of the coffee equipment alone, much less the jarring from being moved from location to location, was easily a disaster waiting to happen.

It felt like a punch in the stomach. This was more than going back to square one. It was a major setback personally, financially, and professionally. Upset, discouraged, and feeling betrayed, Morgan went to the Lord for help to navigate through this new set of problems. She was sure He had brought her this far, so she went back to the landmark of God and His truths to get her bearings and to show her the next steps.

Morgan had the coffee equipment removed and preserved for future use. The trailer was sold for basically the cost of its parts, a fraction of what she had invested in it. All thoughts of moving Cloud 9, as she had known it, to Valencia's Westfield Mall were dashed. Morgan went back to her life verse which says, "And we know that in all things God works for the good of those who love him, who have been called according to his purpose" (Romans 8:28). God was getting ready to work all things for good and bring Morgan back to her original dream of having a brick and mortar coffee shop!

About the same time all of these things were coming to light, Morgan was approached by the people who run the real estate dealings at Stockdale Towers. This twelve-story office complex is where she had established a consistent business with her mobile unit for the first two years. They wanted to begin talking and possibly negotiating lease of a space within the building's ground floor that would enable the tenants of the building to continue to enjoy the delicious coffee, tea, and treats that they had become accustomed to having on the premises.

The negotiated space had been empty for years, so Morgan was able to procure an amazing deal. Her original dream, the desire of her heart, had been to have a brick-and-mortar coffee shop. God was taking the disappointment of a failed venture and was using it to fulfill her deep-seated yearnings. She signed the lease and was excited, expecting to open in a couple of months!

God was not through with her yet! Instead of 2 months, it was a year from the signing of the lease to opening day. Morgan remembers thinking, "If this is what God really wants for me, why is it so hard?" She also knew that she could not rush God or move out of His will, so she began prayerfully waiting on Him. Morgan says she is not a very patient person. Waiting for permits, approvals, and work to be completed was frustrating at times. She described this year of delayed anticipation as both the worst year and the best year of her life.

The worst part was that she felt like she was being given a time out. Children hate sitting in time out, and often mope and pout about it. The purpose is to give them a chance to reflect on their behavior and settle down long enough to work at changing it. While in the midst of waiting, Morgan had time on her hands. She began researching best business practices. She reflected on the type of boss she had been and ways to better relate to her employees. She discovered better ways to treat customers, infusing them with a sense of genuine value. God knew what was necessary to prepare Morgan for the next step in her dream!

God also was able to prove His faithfulness to this newly-wed couple. It was a tough year financially, living on Carter's paychecks alone. Morgan's only source of income was temporarily on hold. She was putting more money into the building of the new space. Morgan smiled as she said, "The Lord always provided. Often it was at the last minute, but things would fall into place. If God gave us everything we asked for, when we asked for it, we wouldn't need to rely on Him." She likened her trust lessons to the Israelites stepping into the Jordan River **before** the waters parted.

The Jordan River was at flood stage when God told Joshua that they would need to prepare to cross to the other side. The priests carrying the Ark of the Covenant went before the people. As soon as their feet touched the river's edge, the water from upstream stopped flowing. They didn't wait until the waters were parted. They knew God had provided for Moses by parting the Red Sea. This was now an act of faith that God would again see them to the other side of an impossible situation. The step of faith opened up the way and allowed the entire throng of Israelites to pass through.

Morgan has continued to step in faith. The store is open and it is a welcoming, warm, and inviting place to sit and sip on a cup of your favorite coffee or tea. It is a place ordained by God. Even the contractor and subcontractors whom she hired had prayed over the space as they worked on it. In the first month of being open, Cloud 9 brought in more sales than the entire 2018 year! Morgan is encouraged and grateful for all that God taught her and the way He navigated her to this new destination.

God moves in our lives to bring glory to His name. Morgan's hope is that Cloud 9 can be an environment in which people feel loved and drawn to her Savior. By showing sincere interest in the welfare of others, by living out a life of joy and peace that others can see, and by owning a business that is covered in prayer, she hopes that people will want to know the God she serves. Her prayer and vision is that Cloud 9 will be a safe harbor for people who walk through its doors and that her Rock, Jesus, will be the landmark that leads them safely to shore.

Soil-Sifting Summary

- The Rock of God is our shelter and our   dwelling place.
- God is our defense.
- We can hide in the shade and the shadow of the Almighty Rock.
- God, as our Rock, is immovable, everlasting, strong, and abiding. He is unchanging; there is no God like our God.
- We must build our lives on God's words, putting them into practice. When we do that we will remain sure-footed. Our foundation will remain solid and true.
- If we lose our way or are uncertain of the direction to head, God will lead and guide us to the right destination. He is our constant and perfect Navigational Aide.
- We don't always understand why things are happening the way they are, but God has a plan to take everything in our lives and work them for His purpose and good.
- Our steps of faith open up the way and allow God to see us to the other side of an impossible situation.

Digging into God's Word

- Psalm 61:2-4
- Psalm 90:1
- Psalm 18:2-3
- Psalm 91:1
- 1 Samuel 2:2
- Hebrews 13:8
- Matthew 7:24-27
- Psalm 31:3
- Romans 8:28

• Joshua 3

Extracting Truths and Treasures

Chapter 2

OUR MIGHTY ROCK

He alone is my rock and my salvation; he is my fortress, I will
not be shaken. Psalm 62:6

$\mathcal{I}$ recently had a chance to visit Mount Rushmore
National Memorial for the first time. The sculpture of the
four presidents carved into the granite face of Mount Rushmore is
an awe-inspiring site. The incredible vision and design of Gutzon
Borglum for this project in the Black Hills of South Dakota is
astounding. It took fourteen years to complete, with the
engineering and technology of the time being a far cry from 21st
century advances. The carvings were meant to represent the birth,
growth, development and preservation of the United States. More
than two million tourists visit each year. It is a rock worth
witnessing.

Nestled in the Black Hills, about six miles from Mount Rushmore
National Memorial, there is the most amazing campground. It is the
KOA Mt. Rushmore Resort and Lodge at Palmer Gulch. The grounds
offer RV sites, tent sites, cabins of all types and sizes, and a
gorgeous lodge. You can use it as your home base for exploring
Mount Rushmore, the Black Hills, Custer State Park, and the
Badlands of South Dakota, or you can keep busy on the grounds
throughout the day. There are large grassy areas for relaxing or
recreation. The camp provides dining alternatives, horseback
riding, and a "Fun Zone" that offers a climbing wall, waterslides,
mini golf and more. This multi-acre property is bordered by
ponderosa pines, leaving you feeling peaceful and protected.

It was in this beautiful setting that I met Taylor. Taylor was with a group called the Summer Shiners, Christian college students who come from all over the United States to live, work and play at various family oriented campgrounds for the summer. They work as paid staffers each day, then use their own time and talents for ministry opportunities: performing skits, directing family-friendly activities, and leading casual Sunday morning worship services. As we were planning our week of fun, we decided we would take part in the Sunday service.

Sunday morning came, and several families joined us on the log-hewn benches facing an outdoor stage. We enjoyed being lead in a few worship songs and watching the kids head up to the front for a Biblical object lesson. The group of five college students took turns praying or reading a passage of Scripture. When it was time for the "sermon," Taylor came to the microphone, which was only working when she held the mic cord at a strategic angle. Regardless of the technical issues, she began to captivate us with her testimony.

The peripheral noise of the other campers seemed to fade away as we were mesmerized by Taylor's story. As a high school sophomore, Taylor started falling asleep in class. She experienced increasingly stiff muscle pain and she couldn't seem to keep any food down. After months of going to doctors, tests of all kinds, and frustrating non-diagnoses, Taylor and her parents found themselves in a clinic room where the doctor told them she had Myelodysplastic Syndrome (MDS). This is a rare blood disorder that four in a million children get. It is essentially pre-leukemia. She had been living with a blood count of eight instead of a normal fourteen, and she would need a bone-marrow transplant. While her parents seemed to be holding back tears and trying to process the information, Taylor was holding back a giggle as the doctor shared about what was going on in her body.

The night before, Taylor had sunk to the floor of the tub sobbing, letting her tears mingle with the shower water. She knew they would be hearing the results of her bone marrow biopsy the next day, and she was preparing herself for the "C" word, cancer. She was exhausted emotionally and physically, but she was also relieved that they were going to get an answer. She hadn't been imagining her pain. She wasn't crazy! Along with the tears, prayers flowed from her heart and soul for herself, her doctors, her family, and for her faith to be strengthened.

So instead of being told it was the cancer she had prepared herself for, she was hearing about some weird disease she had never heard of and that it was...CURABLE! The smile that began to form on her lips wasn't because she had no fears. She certainly was nervous about the needles that were to come, the uncertainty of what would happen to her schooling, and what the treatment protocols would entail. Her stifled laugh was because she knew she was going to be okay, she was going to live. She knew the Lord had her in His hands!!!

It was by no means an easy road. There were hundreds of blood transfusions, over seventy-five medicines, and fifteen bone marrow biopsies. There were several procedures, a donor, and a bone marrow transplant. She got to know scores of amazing doctors and fabulous nurses. She experienced millions of answered prayers offered by thousands of prayer warriors and incredible friends. She was supported by her loving family and received a trillion blessings (Taylor's words). She drew closer to Jesus and came to understand His sacrifice on the cross in a whole new way. During the months of clinging to life and thinking about death, Taylor realized there was no point in living if she wasn't doing so for God. Taylor's life was saved, in more ways than one.

Taylor made a great analogy between her bone marrow transplant and what God did for her (and every single one of us). Her physical blood was not effective, it didn't give her what she needed. She was left feeling tired and empty. Her donor was her dad, her earthly father giving her his "clean, good, perfect" blood which replaced her "bad, dirty, imperfect" blood. Jesus did this same thing for us when He died on the cross. He replaced our unfulfilling, "bad," blood with his perfect, clean, fulfilling blood, the blood of the Lamb.

We were still listening with rapt attention, even as the sun was beginning to heat up and the day was calling us to come play. Taylor was not quite done. As she brought us up to the present day, she shared that through her college years, she continued to nail down her commitment to Christ through some ups and downs. She doubted herself and allowed herself to believe lies that she wasn't enough, that she couldn't be used by God, for God.

In His faithfulness, God gave Taylor a promise, at a time when her anxiety was at its worst. "Find rest, O my soul, in God alone; my hope comes from him. He alone is my rock and my salvation; he is my fortress, I will not be shaken. My salvation and my honor depend on God; he is my mighty rock, my refuge. Trust in him at all times, O people; pour out your hearts to him, for God is our refuge" (Psalm 62:5-8). These verses became her anthem, and a reminder to herself that when she is scared or anxious or worried, she can rest in God as her refuge. He is in control and can be depended on through all of our pain and emotions, decisions and plans.

The day we were hearing Taylor's testimony was six years and two days after the anniversary of her initial diagnosis. Her mom had shared a Facebook memory that had popped up the previous day. In her post she was praising God for the miracle of Taylor's full recovery and the people who had helped them through that trying time in their lives. In the message she had posted six years prior, her mom had claimed Psalm 62:5-8. This promise had given her mom comfort and confidence in God the Rock, just as he had given Taylor that same verse to keep her going through her college days. Taylor was blown away by the way God had woven His wonderful assurance of hope through her life in so many ways.

As we sat among the grandeur of the rock formations of the Black Hills, South Dakota, God was reminding us to trust in Him as our mighty rock, our fortress, our refuge! In Him we find the **solid ground** for establishing our hope. Taylor and I have kept in communication. After finishing her senior year in college, she spent 6 months in Costa Rica doing missions work. God used her greatly and taught her so many lessons during her time there. She started a blog called Hope Abounding. Her theme verse for her blog is Romans 15:13, which says, "May the God of hope fill you with all peace and joy as you trust in Him, so that you may overflow with hope by the power of the Holy Spirit." We had not talked about it, but I had chosen that same passage as my theme during the year I wrote *Common Ground*. Once again God was binding two hearts through His words of hope!

Soil-Sifting Summary

- Jesus exchanged our unfulfilling, "bad," blood with his perfect, clean, fulfilling blood, the blood of the Lamb.
- God is our refuge. He is in control and can be depended on through all of our pain and emotions, decisions and plans.
- God weaves His assurances and binds our hearts through His words of hope.

Digging into God's Word

- I John 1:7
- Psalm 62:5-8
- Romans 15:13

Extracting Truths and Treasures

Chapter 3
WHO IS THE ROCK?

For who is God besides the Lord? And who is the Rock except our God? It is God who arms me with strength and makes my way perfect. He makes my feet like the feet of a deer; he enables me to stand on the heights. Psalm 18:31-33

My sister, Jaleen, is older than me by 18 months. Growing up she was my rock. She taught me to read before kindergarten. She took her piano lessons before me so that I could hear the songs and play them by ear instead of reading the music notes. She kept me level when my emotions got the better of me. She listened to my problems and tried to fix them for me. We shared a room, lots of giggles, and each other's secrets.

Jaleen was definitely a great role model. She was smart, talented, and pretty. She loved the Lord early in life, and her example made me want to serve Jesus. She was very particular about the boyfriends she allowed into her life, and her standards were always high. When she married Mark Morgan, she did well!

Mark pursued a career in the field of medicine. He decided to focus in the area of Obstetrics and Gynecology. He attended medical school at Oklahoma University College of Medicine and did a four year residency there. In his fourth year of med school he did an internship at Kern Medical Center in Bakersfield. Since we lived in Bakersfield, Mark stayed with us for the six weeks of his rotation. We saw very little of him since he got up early and was home late from his shifts. When he did have some time off, we would get together for meals, sometimes with other family members that lived in town. We all remember laughing hysterically as he related some of the stories from his residency experiences. Besides spinning a great tale, he was a great man of God! Plus he loved my sister!

Mark stayed at Oklahoma University and did a two year fellowship specializing in Maternal/Fetal Medicine. From Oklahoma City, he moved to Orange, California to practice, teach, and do research at the University of California, Irvine. Eventually their family moved to Philadelphia, Pennsylvania where he worked as the Director of Maternal Fetal Medicine at the Hospital of the University of Pennsylvania. Life seemed to be going swimmingly. Mark had a successful career. He and Jaleen had two children, a boy and a girl. They had a beautiful house where Jaleen could be a stay-at-home mom. She seemed to have the perfect existence.

On Wednesday, April 15, 1998, her world, as she knew it, was about to abruptly change. My sister, my rock, was rocked with the news that her husband had been diagnosed with pancreatic cancer. For those who have experienced a critical illness involving yourself or a loved one, you can relate to how it takes you down to basics and a dependence on God for healing, strength, and daily hope.

Their daughter was then eleven years old and their son was fourteen. As they received the news, they all held each other and cried. They reflected on how blessed they had been so far in life. Due to Mark's medical background, he understood he would only be healed by a miracle from God, and that is how they prayed. Their family was the recipient of so much love, prayer, and caring from extended family, friends, and Mark's medical colleagues. This support buoyed them up and carried them through these hard times. A couple of friends arranged for Mark to play a round of golf between his treatments. He actually made a hole in one that day. It was God's ways of letting him meet one of his life-long goals early.

After a Whipple procedure (a complex and risky surgery used to treat pancreatic cancer), radiation, chemo, and various clinical trials, Mark passed away on Easter Sunday, April 4, 1999, almost a year from his cancer diagnosis. He had fought a valiant, hard battle and the Lord took him to Heaven on one of the most glorious days of the Christian calendar, Easter Sunday. He was forty-one years old at the time.

During the months of his illness, Mark began to say to his family, "Jesus Has A Plan." Those were his words of hope to them even as he knew he wasn't getting better. They actually had those words etched on his grave marker, and the kids and Jaleen clung to those words after he was gone. They were left with a huge ache and gaping hole in their lives, but God's faithfulness continued to be evident!

My sister and I recently were at an uncle's memorial service. We began reflecting about God's goodness in our lives. She shared with me some things that happened in the year following Mark's passing that I had forgotten about. God's presence was so close that year and through all the grief and tears, she felt His love and guidance each and every day. She truly came to understand God as the Good Shepherd, and Jaleen said, "I was, without a doubt, the sheep. Even though all the props of my life felt kicked out from under me, when everything was stripped away, I sensed such a deep love from God and He was so close in my decision making that I actually heard his voice almost audibly at times as I sought daily guidance." When she felt like she was drifting deep into despairing grief, she would land on the **solid ground** of God's incredible, unfailing love.

As she waded through paperwork, financial decisions and connecting with a new career path as an elementary music teacher, she trusted God for open and closed doors. Even though it felt at times she was walking in the dark, God's guidance would break through at just the right time to actually show her the way. He would give her confirmation of what to do next, one day at a time. She experienced God's protection and safety steadying her in the storm.

She shared three specific stories illustrating God's guidance during this time. I feel like it is best to let you read it straight from her words. The first of these special gifts from God happened like this:

> There were some insurance disability papers that needed to be signed by Mark's oncologist. One morning I got the kids off to school and clearly heard instructions and prodding from God to go to the hospital that particular day. I argued with God a bit, but finally left the house for the long commute. I went up to the appointment desk and the secretary there told me to go down one floor to the business office. I was just explaining what I needed when the business person said, "Why, there's the doctor now! He usually is not down here because he is seeing patients all day. You are really lucky!" Luck...I don't think so. The doctor signed the papers right then and I thanked the Lord for his perfect timing and guidance!

The next incident occurred as the first Christmas without Mark was approaching. It was understandably a struggle. She explained,

I knew I still had to focus on the kids, so I forced myself to go to the mall and was feeling sorry for myself. Walking to the counter to make my final purchase, there was an elderly lady and her friend in front of me. She was sharing with her friend how excited she was to be well enough to shop and be out of the house. You could feel her positive energy, and I was right behind her in line. After her purchase was made, she turned and you could see that huge portions of her face were marred and flesh was eaten away, probably by cancer or burns, and yet it had not dampened her joyful spirit one bit! I began to cry as I headed for my car and thanked the Lord for placing me there at just the right time. God showed me it was time to abandon my own "pity party." There is suffering all around us!

The last event centered on the pursuing of her new career. It happened like this:

As part of going back to school to complete class work for my music education certification, I was required to do several observations and had to set these up on my own. I was driving past a middle school near my children's school district when it felt like God stopped me dead in my tracks and clearly told me (as if he was speaking) that I needed to schedule an observation at that exact school. I did, and my first job a year or so later turned out to be as a long term substitute teacher at that very school. Coincidence? I don't believe so!

During our trials, we tend to cling to certain passages of scripture. As Jaleen read and claimed God's truth each day, she would tell herself– PRAY, Don't PANIC, be POSITIVE and follow God's PLAN. Several verses were especially meaningful to Jaleen during this time:

"Do not be anxious about anything, but in everything by prayer and petition, with thanksgiving, present your requests to God. And the peace of God, which transcends all understanding, will guard your hearts and your minds in Christ Jesus" (Philippians 4:6-7).

"So do not fear, for I am with you; do not be dismayed, for I am your God. I will strengthen you and help you; I will uphold you with my righteous right hand" (Isaiah 41:10).

"Find rest, O my soul, In God alone; my hope comes from him. He alone is my rock and my salvation; he is my fortress, I will not be shaken. My salvation and my honor depend on God; he is my mighty rock, my refuge. Trust in him at all times, O people; pour out your hearts to him, for God is our refuge" (Psalm 62:5-8).

When Jaleen was feeling like the ground was falling away, God carried and guided her and placed her on **solid ground**. Who was the Rock? Not Jaleen, not Mark, not any human on this earth, for that matter. Others come alongside us, for sure, but God is the one who arms us with strength and enables us to stand on the heights (Psalm 18:32-33). He has continued to heal, comfort, and restore. Fast forward twenty years—God has blessed her with a wonderful husband, Joel Rayburn, who God has sent into her life to help watch over her. That's a story for another time.

Soil-Sifting Summary

- Jesus has a plan!
- God is our Good Shepherd!
  - God steadies us in the midst of the storm.
- PRAY, Don't PANIC, be POSITIVE and follow God's PLAN.
- Who is the Rock? Others may come alongside us, for sure, but God is the one who arms us with strength and enables us to stand on the heights.

Digging into God's Word

- Jeremiah 29:11
- John 10:14
- Psalm 107:28-31
- Philippians 4:6-7
- Psalm 62:5-8
- Psalm 18:31-33

Extracting Truths and Treasures

_____

_____
_____
_____
_____
_____
_____
_____
_____
_____
_____
_____
_____
_____
_____
_____
_____
_____
_____
_____
_____
_____
_____
_____
_____
_____
_____
_____

Chapter 4
OUR REFUGE AND FORTRESS

I will say of the Lord, "He is my refuge and my fortress, my God, in whom I trust." Psalm 91:2

There are some amazing citadels throughout Europe that have withstood the test of time. One of the most fascinating of these strongholds is the Tower of London. William the Conqueror began building the castle in 1066 to protect himself from attack and to show Londoners that he was boss. Additional stone towers, inner defensive walls, a moat, a water gate, and even a zoo were added throughout the next couple of centuries by succeeding sovereignty. Throughout history, the Tower of London has served as a royal palace, a prison, a place of execution, an arsenal, royal mint, menagerie, and jewel house. Today it is an awesome tourist attraction, but it is still a compelling and imposing fortress and place of refuge.

By definition, a fortress is a person or thing not susceptible to outside influence or disturbance. Refuge means a condition of being safe or sheltered from pursuit, danger, or trouble. As parents and grandparents, we try to protect and shelter our children. We want our homes to be a place of refuge and our arms to be a fortress for them. We know that things will enter their lives that are painful: skinning a knee, feeling rejection from friends, losing a pet. On an even larger scale, there might be a devastating injury or illness, deep sorrow and grief over a lost loved one, or relentless bullying by a peer. We do our best to be there for our children, to provide a safe place for them to rest. We work with doctors, counselors, or teachers to help remedy situations that are bringing them harm or danger beyond our immediate control.

Even with our best efforts, we fall short. Eventually they grow up, and we have to let them go. We have to put them in God's hands. That's why it's important to teach them about God's provisions for their lives when they are young. When we teach them to consider God as their refuge and fortress, they are learning to trust in Him to protect them from danger and harm. Together we look to Him as One who is more powerful than any enemy that might try to assail us. We can count on His promises to be with us in trouble, to deliver and honor us.

Greg and Myrna Gebhart had built this type of foundation, this **solid ground**, of love, discipline, and knowledge for their kids. Growing up in a pastor's home is not always easy. Their daughter, Charity, had not been happy about their recent move to Fresno. She was maneuvering her way through junior high and trying to be accepted by a whole new group of friends. In her later high school years she began to drift away from God's plan. In the midst of all of this she found herself criticized and "judged" by comments made by some of the church members. Oh, how much better off we would all be if we would pray for those we might disapprove of and love them into God's kingdom rather than to gossip and assess their behavior.

Charity graduated from high school, went through beauty school, and was finding success styling hair at a prestigious salon. She had become involved with a young man, and was intent on marrying him, even though the relationship was not a healthy one. He had broken up with her over the phone, so she had made a trip to Santa Cruz to try to "fix" things. As she was heading back to Fresno on the morning of January 16, 2003, she was in a state of uncertainty. Somewhere along Highway 152 Charity slowed down to navigate through a patch of fog. It had come on suddenly, with visibility of only one hundred feet. Unseen to her, a tanker truck made a right turn at an intersection right in front of her. The only thing she could do was hit the brakes and crank the steering wheel to the right to try to avoid under riding the truck's trailer. She slammed into the vehicle's rear axles. The tanker continued to roll over the hood of her new Ford Mustang. The front of the car was crushed, which caused the driver's side door to buckle.

Realizing she had dodged possible death, Charity's first thoughts were that God was giving her a second chance. She then looked over at the console and was able to grab her phone. Though it was partially broken apart by the impact, she was somehow able to make a call. When her dad didn't answer, she urgently attempted to dial her mom's number. Myrna answered what sounded like a prank call. There was static and a sound like labored breathing. She was about to hang up when God prompted her to ask, "Charity, is that you?" She heard a feeble yes. She then asked, "Have you been in an accident?" To that question, she received another raspy affirmation.

Just the day before, Myrna had been praying for Charity. She and Greg had moved temporarily into a condominium due to a job change. As she was unpacking a box in the downstairs bathroom, Charity's bathroom, she came across a sun catcher with the verse from Psalm 91:11, "For he will command his angels concerning you to guard you in all your ways." Myrna was impressed by the Holy

Spirit to begin fervently praying the words of this passage over her daughter. The very next day she was going to see the fulfillment of this promise.

As Myrna kept Charity on the phone, she began to hear another voice. Charity told her a man was at her car door to help her. The door was jammed and Charity was unable to exit the vehicle. Myrna could hear a bending of metal as this helper literally pried the door off and handled the car's twisted interior to get Charity's foot released. There was no way for her to walk on her foot, which later required surgery, but this man carried her to a safe spot on the side of the road. He then went back to the car and gathered Charity's blanket, pillow, and slippers to help her be as comfortable as possible.

As emergency personnel began to arrive, the man knelt down and told her, "I have to go now. People are coming to help you." The last Charity saw of him was as he walked away and disappeared into the fog. Those who had witnessed the scene never saw anyone but Charity. They claimed she walked to the side of the road, but that would have been physically impossible for her to do. Not only had she been trapped inside the car with an injured foot, but she was physically not strong enough to pry the door open on her own. Charity and Myrna both knew that an angel had been at the scene guarding her ways. God's promise of commanding His angels over us is real and is an assurance to be claimed by His people.

Greg left his meeting, picked up their high school son, and grabbed Myrna from home. As they started toward the scene of the accident, they received a call from the paramedics instructing them to meet at Madera Hospital. They were there when the ambulance and the on-duty California Highway Patrol (CHP) officer arrived. An off-duty CHP officer who had come upon the scene of the accident had stated that Charity had walked herself to the side of the road. It was now quite evident to the on-duty officer that with her injuries there was no way she would have been able to walk. Myrna told him that she believed someone with supernatural powers had assisted her daughter. Greg turned to the CHP officer and said, "God is good." The officer replied, "All the time." He then declared, "Mr. and Mrs. Gebhart, it sounds like an angel pulled your daughter from that wreckage to save her life." Knowing that this CHP officer shared their belief in Almighty God gave the Gebhart's great comfort and added to their confidence that God was in control.

X-rays showed that her left foot had been shattered and would require surgery. The other foot had no broken bones, but tendons and muscles had been twisted and stretched to the point she could put no weight on it. Charity kept complaining about her arm. For some reason the doctor didn't immediately have the arm x-rayed, but when he finally did, the image revealed that her right arm was completely broken in two. With her opposite arm and foot out of commission, it was next to impossible for Charity to mobilize herself, but the ER doctor sent her home with directions to make an appointment with an orthopedic surgeon.

Greg and his firefighter nephew who had shown up at the hospital, helped get Charity in the car. They called ahead to get an appointment with the specialist, and they were headed that way. Since Charity had not had anything to eat all morning, and it was now well into the afternoon, they stopped at a Jamba Juice. When they got to the Kaiser facility, the surgeon they had made the appointment with was a graduate from Point Loma Nazarene University. God was placing people in their path that gave them assurance and support. He said she definitely needed surgery and that he could do it, but since she had eaten something they were going to have to wait until the next morning.

They got a wheelchair to transport her, set her up in her downstairs bedroom in their condo, and prepared for a night-time vigil. Charity was now home with her broken bones in splints and some pain medication prescribed by the doctor. Myrna slept fitfully while Greg sat by Charity's side. When she would awaken, Myrna found herself doubting that it really was an angel that had been at the scene. The next morning, the phone was ringing off the hook as people were checking in on Charity's progress, giving comfort and prayer support. While on the phone with one of her friends, another call came in. Myrna said she clicked over and the voice of what sounded like an operator of some kind said to her, "Yes, God does send his angels down to protect us." The phone call ended. She was back talking to her friend, excitedly explaining what had just happened and praising God. God definitely wanted Myrna to stay strong and trust in Him, and He was providing the exact type of love, support, and affirmation that she needed.

What normally would have given Charity relief and helped her to sleep, when taken on an empty stomach the pain meds caused her to start throwing up. She began to get dehydrated and weak. On top of it all, the surgeon called the next morning saying he had come down sick and he was unable to do the surgery. Within about an hour of this call, the Gebharts realized that Charity was failing quickly! They called 911. Her veins had collapsed and the paramedics couldn't get an IV started. They finally just moved her into their vehicle to get her to the hospital as quickly as they could. The Emergency Room was completely full, with no rooms available.

Charity was listlessly waiting on a gurney in the hallway with her mom and brother standing by her side, feeling helpless. Suddenly a doctor came through the doors. He was the head of the cardiology department and had obvious clout in the hospital. He took one look at Charity's skin coloring, and he began ordering personnel to move quickly, clear a room, and get her taken care of NOW. Myrna just began praying that they would be able to get an IV in her. They finally were successful, but the following few hours were really touch-and-go. They didn't know what was going to happen, but they realized that this cardiologist was another God-send. Who knows what might have happened if he had not walked through the doors at just that moment. Charity's organs were beginning to fail, and that night was a critical time for her. The cardiologist stayed on her case the entire eight days she was in the hospital to see her through.

Once Charity stabilized a bit, they were finally able to do the surgery on her foot and set her arm. Each day they were finding more issues related to the accident and the trauma it had placed on Charity. In the following four months Myrna took care of Charity as best she could. Myrna remembered that as hard as it was at times, God's grace was always sufficient. When we are at our weakest point, God's power can be revealed.

When Myrna had a chance to look more closely at the angel verse God had given her, she was amazed at what she found. She noticed how specifically God had spoken through her scripture-prayer. The verse following the one on the sun catcher says, "They will lift you up in their hands so that you will not strike your foot against a stone" (Psalm 91:12). The angel had literally lifted Charity up out of the car and placed slippers on her feet to protect them. Charity had been lifted out of her physical brokenness, but more importantly out of her spiritual brokenness.

Over time, Charity has continued to improve. She is now running her own daycare business in her home. She is married, has two great boys, and loves the Lord. She is doing everything she knows to give her own kids a safe harbor through their home and through her church family. She and her mom are using her story to help Charity's boys and others learn about God, their refuge and fortress.

Soil-Sifting Summary

- It's important to teach our children about God's provisions for their lives when they are young.
- When we consider God as our refuge and fortress, we are trusting in Him to protect us from harm. We look to Him as One who is more powerful than any enemy that might try to assail us. We count on His promises to be with us in trouble, to deliver and honor us.
- Oh, how much better off we would all be if we would pray for those we might disapprove of and love them into God's kingdom rather than to gossip and assess their behavior.
- God's promise of commanding His angels over us is real and is an assurance to be claimed by His people.
- When we are at our weakest point, God's power can be revealed.
- We can teach our children and others about how God is our refuge and fortress through our own stories

Digging into God's Word

- Proverbs 22:6
- Psalm 91:14-16
- Romans 14:9-13
- Psalm 91:11-12
- 2 Corinthians 12:9-10
- Psalm 91:1-2

Extracting Truths and Treasures

Chapter 5
EQUIPPED

May the God of peace...equip you with everything good for doing
his will, and may he work in us what is pleasing to him, through
Jesus Christ, to whom be glory for ever and ever. Amen.
Hebrews 13:20-21

𝔐organ Smith, or Pastor Moe, as our teens called
him, is full of energy and enthusiasm. He loves the Lord
with all his heart, soul, mind, and strength. He loves his wife and
two precious little ones. He puts his all into his ministry with
teenagers, remembering some of the struggles he faced during
those vulnerable years. One of the things Moe has learned is the
importance of having the right equipment. Having the right
paraphernalia for various life endeavors provides a great object
lesson for why believers in Jesus need the full armor of God in order
to face the devil's schemes.

When he surfs, he knows the importance of having a good
surfboard. Caring for it is as important as riding the waves on it, so
it is crucial to rinse off the salt water, fix any dings, and keep it
covered and protected. Wearing a good wetsuit to protect yourself
from cold and sun is part of the package deal, and keeping your
surfboard on a leash so you don't lose it in the water is the only
sensible way to go.

Along with surfing, one of Moe's passions is rock climbing.
Moe's love for rock climbing began at Camp Oakhurst. He worked
on the ropes team at the camp during the summers, helping

campers make their way through the high-ropes course. The staff would do small rock climbs on their days off in the Yosemite Valley, which really piqued his interest in the sport. The "bug" really bit him when he went to Nazarene Bible College in Colorado Springs, CO. Rock climbing became his exclusive sport, a way to challenge himself, release tension, and practice positive self-talk to get through the tough moments. It became a spiritual connection for him as well, as he was able to be out in the wilderness, in God's creation. He recognized that he could remain on the **solid ground** of God's Word and His faithfulness even when hundreds of feet above the earth's floor.

Over time, Moe began to connect with a group of guys who also loved the sport. One of the nice things about it was that you really only need one other person to go with you, to be your belay partner. He would grab one of his friends, head out to "a climb," and hone his skills. The discipline to keep going, to make it to the top, required concentration, muscle memory and stamina. Part of the experience was a mandatory, overwhelming, positive attitude every time he would go to climb. You had to be "super psyched," as Moe put it. Any negative thoughts, loss of focus, or allowing your mind to go to the wrong place, would be the end of the route.

The art of staying laser focused trickled down into his spiritual life as well. Just as he gave each climb his complete attention and effort, Moe began to develop a greater discipline of giving God his all. Moe admits to having a little Attention-Deficit-Hyperactivity-Disorder (ADHD). In school, while in math class, his mind would take him fishing. He acknowledges he is a little all over the place, and it doesn't come naturally to him to keep his mind centered on one thing. Climbing helped him to learn about being present in the moment.

From the middle of the Rockies in Colorado to some of Moe's favorite climbs in Yosemite, this sport opened up amazing opportunities for him. One of his favorite climbs was a 1600 foot climb in Yosemite called the Royal Arches at the base of the grand Ahwahnee Hotel. He tackled this fete with his friend John. It was their first "big-wall" climb, which is a climb that is anything over 1000 feet. They studied the guide book, became completely familiar with the route, and knew every single pitch. They had it mapped out as to who would lead each pitch, a section of the rock that was about a rope's length. One of them would climb the section, placing the equipment into the rock as they went, trusting their partner to belay them. Once at the belay station, the other partner would follow, picking up the equipment as he went, trusting the person at the top to belay him. They would alternate the responsibilities to the top.

Though the climbing was fairly easy, the distance was like a marathon. Looking up from the base was both daunting and exhilarating. Moe was reminded of the scripture that says, "...let us throw off everything that hinders and the sin that so easily entangles, and let us run with perseverance the race marked out for us" (Hebrews 12:1b). Moe and John knew they would have to possess perseverance. They would need to prevent all distractions or diversions from hindering their course. Keeping the goal in mind, they paced themselves, let other groups pass them, and stayed with the plan that they had so carefully laid out.

It was one of the scariest and most rewarding climbs Moe remembers. Looking down at the ground below him, the trees looked like toothpicks. At that point his climbing focus and prayer focus became married, as they knew it would be disastrous if anything went wrong at this height. It might have been easy to stop at 1000 feet, knowing that they had conquered a big wall climb. They were no longer in the protection of the trees and surrounding rock formations. They were being buffeted by stronger and stronger winds, exposed to all of the elements. But they kept their eye on the goal, and kept going.

Again, there was a spiritual connection. We get comfortable with our Christian friends, at church, at camp, surrounded by the protective forces of the body of Christ. When we leave and go back to the real world—work, school, life—we are exposed to the devil's schemes. It is then that we need to truly keep our focus on "...Jesus, the author and perfecter of our faith" (Hebrews 12:2a).

Moe and John made it to the top. The beauty of God's creation from that vantage point exceeded anything they had known up to this point in time. Their smallness compared to the huge rock put God's greatness into perspective. The destination was amazing, but the process of getting there was what they will always remember. Tapping into their reserve energy, energy they didn't even think they had, was part of the journey. The stories of their trek were interspersed with trials and challenges.

As prepared as they were for this climb, one of the things they didn't account for was how much water they would need. Before reaching the top they had run out of water. They were literally licking the rock to get a bit of water that was streaming down the precipice crags. Certain that they would come home with some parasitic disease, they had to weigh whether they wanted to die of dehydration now or suffer stomach issues later. They learned from that experience to take more water and to pack more efficiently.

It had taken Moe a decade to acquire all the needed equipment for doing a variety of climbs. He was able to use his equipment for his first sermon illustration at his new church in San Luis Obispo. He had just moved from Bakersfield to San Luis Obispo as youth pastor. In order for the congregation to get to know him a little better, he preached a sermon shortly after starting there. He brought all of his rock-climbing gear on stage. He connected the tools we need for a successful climb with the tools we are given for a successful life. Sometimes we choose not to use them. We would rather use the little saw on our pocket knife instead of the power saw that God has provided. He has placed people and promises in our path that we can hang onto in order to have a successful walk with God.

Just as we learn from those who have faith in Jesus, climbers learn from each other. There is an immediate comradery and connection between fellow climbers. They sit around camp at night telling of their experiences. They relive their epic moments and tell about the holds that they were able to accomplish even though they were just about done physically. They also tell of the mistakes and near horrors of their climbs. Whether the successes or the close calls, the stories they share help guide each other. They learn from each other the way they want to go, and they are warned about which routes or treacheries to avoid. They encourage each other to stick to the climbing guide book for the rock they are climbing.

In our spiritual walk, we need to hear each other's stories as well. We can be encouraged to follow the right path, and we can be warned by someone's mistakes to avoid the wrong path. Ultimately, we direct each other to the Guide Book, God's Word. If we deviate from its teachings, we are going to get off course and experience disaster, disappointment, or disillusionment. Let's commit to being all-in, laser-focused, to God and His direction for our lives. Count on the equipment He has provided for us instead of trying to do things our own way. Staying the course, finishing the climb, and embracing the journey will be worth it when we arrive at our heavenly destination!

Soil-Sifting Summary

- Having the right paraphernalia for various life endeavors provides a great object lesson for why believers in Jesus need to put on the full armor of God in order to face the devil's schemes.
- We have to show perseverance and keep from allowing distractions or any diversions from our course to hinder us. Keeping the goal in mind, we must pace ourselves and stay with the plan that God has carefully laid out.
- The real world exposes us to the devil's schemes. It is especially critical in our daily lives to keep our eyes fixed on Jesus.
- He has placed people and promises in our path that we can hang onto in order to have a successful walk with God.
- Ultimately, we direct each other to the Guide Book, God's Word. If we deviate from its teachings, we are going to get off course and experience disaster, disappointment, or disillusionment.

Digging into God's Word

- Ephesians 6:10-18
- Hebrews 12:1-2
- Hebrews 13:20-21
- Psalm 119:105

Extracting Truths and Treasures

Chapter 6
I WILL NOT BE SHAKEN

I have set the Lord always before me. Because he is at my right
hand, I will not be shaken. Psalm 16:8

There are certain things you don't want to hear at the
airport. Right at the top of the list is, "Your flight has
been grounded due to mechanical issues." About the only thing
worse would be to hear there were mechanical issues while in the
air!

On a recent flight to the east coast, we arrived at the terminal to
find that three flights, including ours, had been canceled because of
maintenance problems. In the scramble to reschedule, we found
ourselves in a line with other harried passengers. We were all
attempting to catch a plane that would not delay our trip too
drastically. Since we were in vacation mode, our time and itinerary
were pretty flexible. Others were on a tighter time frame, needing
to arrive for business purposes. The lady in front of us was between
angry and frantic. She was supposed to be at the White House that
evening, and she had already arranged and paid for her Uber ride
from Dulles National Airport. We talked a bit and shared the
customer service number with her that we had been given. She was
able to procure a direct flight on a different airline that would allow
her to reach her destination in a timely manner.

Ten days later, we were heading home. To my surprise the same
lady we had met in line on day one slipped into the window seat
beside me. She was quite inebriated, but somehow sensed that this

second encounter was not a coincidence. She chattered for a couple of hours about the importance of her work, her political leanings, and her faith in God. I tried to gently listen and respond with kindness and truth.

A few cups of coffee and an hour nap helped to turn the tide in her clarity of mind and speech. During the last hour of the flight, we had a deep conversation that changed both of our lives. Lydia, the anonymous name of my new friend, runs a nonprofit organization that advocates for women's rights, specifically seeking to help young women find avenues of opportunity in STEM (Science, Technology, Engineering, and Math) fields. She speaks nationally and globally, with a variety of public and political figures, to try to change the way humans treat each other. Lydia, I found out, accepted the Lord in her teenage years. She tries to run her business each day by asking, "What would Jesus do?" She struggles with conflict personally, spiritually, and politically, as she works to help people understand her platform.

As I listened and shared some of my perspective, Lydia told me about the dream she had while taking her short nap. Her dream had given her a vision of how she could interact with government officials: a true bipartisan discussion where everyone could listen to both sides and come up with solutions together. Our conversation helped her to see that most people want the same thing: unity and respect. She seemed excited about the future. When I asked if I could pray with her, she genuinely received the offer. Our airplane seats became a holy place where we could connect on **solid ground** while flying thousands of feet in the air.

My prayer was simple. I asked for God's protection and guidance with her family, her business, and her personal life. I asked for

God's blessing over her fresh vision. I thanked God for our providential meeting. We held hands and leaned toward each other as our hearts reached out to our Heavenly Father. I'm sure I detected a tear or two in Lydia's eyes, and I know I was moved.

Lydia wanted to exchange phone numbers so she could contact me for occasional prayers when things were ramping up in her life. I gladly agreed, but didn't really think much would come of it. As we were waiting for our luggage, I introduced Lydia to our traveling companions. She beamed as she proclaimed me as her new prayer partner. My commitment was taking on a new level. She seemed serious about this!

I have often heard stories about people meeting on planes and having truly ordained and timely conversations with a seat mate. It had never happened to me before, but God seemed to have a special plan in place. I really wanted to ignore her at first. The flight attendants were sympathetic towards us, and were secretly willing me to feign sleep to get her to quiet down. However, something drew us together!

We have texted several times since that day. I will send her a scripture verse or a particularly good quote from a devotional I have read. She responds with how it seems to be just what she needs for that moment. I always think of her when I'm flying somewhere. On a recent trip to Baltimore I had been praying for her, and planned to text her when we landed. When I changed my phone out of airplane mode, a text appeared from her. She was in a crucial place in her annual planning and needed prayer.

Over the next few weeks we texted, called or emailed back and forth. One alarming text from her went something like this:

Hi Jan, I hope you're doing well! I have a prayer request...January was a tough month financially as so many of our sponsors and funders are government or education, and we experienced extreme payment delays due to the [government] shutdown. Some people had to pull out entirely for the year. I couldn't pay myself the last couple of months, and I can't pay my rent, and even groceries. I haven't experienced this extreme since I was a child. I'm praying for a miracle, donations, ticket sales, anything that will relieve this heavy burden. I work so hard and it's been a paradox of things finally falling into place, and dreams coming true, as well as me not being able to pay my bills. It will pass to be sure, but today I am in fear and tears and worried about losing my home. I spent the entire month walking in faith and feeling like God will take care of me. And yet today that faith is shaken because I still see nothing. I asked God tearfully, how much more can I take? I need a prayer circle, and I'm reaching out to those who can pray for me. I don't want to lose the faith. Thank you!

I emailed her back this note:

First of all, I can't even imagine how hard it is to see your dreams coming true on one hand, yet not see the fruit of it (at least financially) on the other hand. Just know, I am not making light of your physical needs AT ALL! I'm hoping you have some people (church, family, close friends) locally who you can reach out to for help just to see you through. If I lived close, I would so be bringing by sacks of groceries!!!

Second, the word shaken is what really stuck out to me,

when you said in your text, "...yet today my faith is shaken because I still see nothing." My mind went to some Psalms (our mutual fave). Psalm 16:8 says, "I have set the Lord always before me. Because he is at my right hand, I will not be shaken." When you consider what being at someone's right hand meant in Biblical times it had many connotations: 1) being someone's advocate in court; 2) giving support in battle; 3) being a companion for a journey. My encouragement for you today is that God **is** your **advocate,** your **support,** and your **companion** on this journey. Keep putting Him in front of you even when you cannot see the results. That's what faith means. I can tell you still believe that it will come about, you are just in a brief season of doubt, and certainly are experiencing need. Having doubt is normal. It's what we do with it that matters. We can spiral off into despair, or we can use it to strengthen our belief system.

Similarly, Psalm 62:1-2 says, "My soul finds rest in God alone; my salvation comes from him. He alone is my rock and my salvation; he is my fortress, I will never be shaken." David penned this during a time when he was being relentlessly pursued by his enemies. He recognized that he had no strength within himself!

Finally, God said of himself in Isaiah 54:10, "'Though the mountains be shaken and the hills be removed, yet my unfailing love for you will not be shaken nor my covenant of peace be removed,' says the Lord, who has compassion on you." If I were to paraphrase this passage for you, it might say, "Though the financial security be shaken and sponsors and funders be removed, yet my unfailing love for Lydia will not be shaken nor my covenant of peace be removed, says the Lord who has compassion on her (from the minute details of her physical well-being to the huge miracles of her non-profit status)."

May you feel God's compassionate arms around you. I pray that either an opportunity will come knocking at your door today, or you will know who, when and where to seek for assistance. Sometimes God brings us to a place of complete trust and humility so that we can later have an even greater empathy towards the ones we help.

I hope these thoughts, which are sent to you as a prayer, will be an encouragement to your heart and soul today!

She texted met to let me know she had read and reread the email many times and it brought her to tears. Literally two days later she texted this message:

God is GREAT! Today I sealed a partnership to support my foundation in a variety of ways. Among the greatest of these is they will cover our office rent for the entire year!!! That's $30k off my annual budget that I can put back into the company. Plus, I'm moving to a coveted corner office to start fresh. I am grateful for the future provisions and opportunities. Now if God can answer my prayers to cover this month's house rent/bills and groceries. I have $15 on me. A scary position to be in. But it is such a relief to know my future is covered in such a way. I pray for more miracles this week! Thank you for holding space for me and interceding with prayers! God hears us!!!

The next day I received this exciting word from her:

A MIRACLE!!! My Operations Manager is writing me a check for $2500 so I can pay my rent and bills this month. I am in tears! I got the bank to take off the overdraft fees!!! So that's $140 off the negative balance!! I hope you don't mind me sharing these miracles! Our prayers worked!

Of course I didn't mind! All of these answers to prayer were building my faith on the spot! Finally on February 11, ten days after the initial cry for help, I received this email:

Hello Jan,

I have read and reread and reread [your] email multiple times since you've sent it. I was really feeling that sense of defeat and despair. I had been working SO HARD and while there were a variety of wonderful things that were happening, the financial security wasn't there all of a sudden. It was really challenging for me to be in that space for the last several weeks.

I thought about a song I once heard, and then later sang at a retreat:
He gives beauty for ashes
Grace for fear
Gladness for mourning
Peace for despair...

And I sang that to myself to soothe me when I felt weary. There were pockets of moments where I didn't necessarily lose faith—but I felt as though I didn't understand WHY I have walked through those valleys and faced such challenges. That despair really made me withdraw in some ways. I let emails go, and I lost the energy to interact with many people, especially while being sick on top of everything. I felt like I traveled a journey of faith over the last few weeks.

But this email/prayer you sent brought me comfort. Slowly over the last few days miracles have shown up and God has answered...first I was able to negotiate my office space rent to be covered for the entire year! Offsetting $30k off my yearly budget! Then my Operations Manager donated a sum of money that allowed me to cover my rent and bills this month. And I've been negotiating sponsor commitments, and received links to apply to other funds, which deadlines were today! So fingers crossed. And I also heard back from the Mark Cuban fund...so just waiting to actually hear from him directly. I was asked to speak at a prestigious conference, which has been one of my dreams. And we had a trickle of ticket sales start to come in...that I am hoping begins to pour in. I feel a peace in my heart today. I don't have all the answers, but somehow I know that God has my back. :)

Where there are two or more gathered...The power of prayer is strong. Thank you for standing in the gap for me and interceding with prayer.

Yes, there are moments where it feels like my faith is shaken—but God always wakes me up and shakes me harder to remind me that I am always loved and taken care of.

I appreciate you. Thank you for showing up.

You see, God was FOR her all along. Satan was there to discourage and try to shake her foundation. God is the One who showed up and had us meet at just the right time and the right place to encourage each other in the Lord. I know her story and the miracles that she was able to share increased my faith and will remind me that I can count on God to be my fortress and strength, my foundation and my Rock!

Soil-Sifting Summary

- When you consider what being at someone's right hand meant in Biblical times it had many connotations: 1) being someone's advocate in court; 2) giving support in battle; 3) being a companion for a journey. Be encouraged that God **is** your **advocate,** your **support,** and your **companion** on your journey.
- We must recognize that we have no strength within ourselves! It comes from God alone!
- God's unfailing love for you will not be shaken nor His covenant of peace be removed. He has compassion on you!
- He gives beauty for ashes, grace for fear, gladness for mourning, and peace for despair!
- The power of prayer is strong. We need to stand in the gap and intercede for each other with prayer.

Digging into God's Word

- Psalm 16:8-11
- Psalm 62:1-2
- Isaiah 54:10
- Isaiah 61:1-3
- Matthew 18:19-2

Extracting Truths and Treasures

Chapter 7

SUPER POWER

That is why, for Christ's sake, I delight in weaknesses, in insults, in hardships, in persecutions, in difficulties. For when I am weak, then I am strong. 2 Corinthians 12:10

My granddaughter loves superheroes, so it made sense to celebrate her 5th birthday with a superhero party. All of the invited guests wore a superhero cape or mask. If they didn't have one or had forgotten their own, masks were available at the door. Each child imagined that they had a particular super power, and they received extra strength from the superhero cupcakes. The parents captured the "Super Team" in a photo with Gotham City as the backdrop. To cap this theme party off, my son set up an amazing obstacle course in which the preschoolers broke through walls (of cardboard boxes), scaled amazing heights (of a toddler slide), and swooped in to save the baby (a doll) from the villain.

Most of us would love to have super strength and stamina. We desire to get through this life without feeling weak or feeble. We work hard at becoming emotionally, physically, and spiritually strong. The bottom line however, is that "...even youths grow tired and weary, and young men stumble and fall" (Isaiah 40:30). In order to soar like an eagle (see Isaiah 40:31), we have to first be drained and at a low point. We have to be weak in order to gain the power of God.

To many of us, Debbie Burris would seem like a superhero. However, she would neither want to be pitied for her life's trials nor exalted for the strength she has had to endure them. Debbie has just chosen to let God lead her through her life and teach her of His love and strength. When she has needed comfort and the knowledge of God's presence, He has made Himself real to her. Her strength lies in Jesus, and it has been during her lowest moments when this strength has risen.

Debbie and I met at Hume Lake, where we were both attending a wedding. As we talked over breakfast, I realized that Debbie's story was worth telling. We scheduled a meeting later in the morning, and I was both humbled and blessed by her words. She began by sharing about her childhood. She had a strong family who believed in Jesus and went to church every time the doors opened. She accepted Jesus into her life personally, and was striving to live for Him. This **solid ground** foundation drew her closer to Jesus during several pivotal events in her life. The first one happened in her late teens.

Debbie was dating a boy from the youth group. They dated throughout their high school years. Everyone, including Debbie, "knew" they would get married someday. Unfortunately, her boyfriend got involved in the drugs of the 1960's. He was careful around her and didn't include her in his "highs." Debbie did not realize the extent of his addictions until she received a call one night that he had been admitted to the hospital. He had "flipped out" on LSD and was being observed and evaluated in the psychiatric ward. With tears streaming down her face, Debbie cried out to God to save him from the grip of drugs on his life. She knew it was God's will for her boyfriend to be free. She recognized his talents and gifts that could be used greatly for God. What she couldn't understand is why her prayers seemed to hit the ceiling. She did not feel like God was listening to her cries.

Eventually, Debbie stilled her frenzied requests long enough to hear God's voice. Her prayer changed to, "God, please heal him, even if it means ending the relationship." It became clear that God was asking her to break up with her boyfriend. She struggled with God. Surely her boyfriend needed her to help him through this time. Certainly there would be no one else who would truly love her like he did. This couldn't be what God really wanted. Eventually, she stopped her arguments and rationale and agreed to end the relationship. Immediately, she felt a sense of peace. She felt like the heavens opened up and that God was holding her. His word to her was that her boyfriend would be fine. She fell into a restful sleep.

The next morning she went to the hospital with her parents. Her boyfriend was calm and clear- headed. Debbie was typically the one who calmed him, and he had been paranoid of everyone else. On this morning, it was just the opposite. As soon as she sat next to him, he became agitated and confused. It was a confirmation that she needed to stop seeing him so that God could heal him and work in his life. It was time to let him go. Debbie was convinced it was the right thing to do, but she also believed she would never find anyone else.

God did not leave her nor forsake her. Within a few months she met the man who would eventually become her husband of 46 years. She met Ron at work in May. They dated for a few months, were engaged in July, and he joined the navy in October. They were married in December, between boot camp and his deployment to Viet Nam. He was supposed to come home in April, but wasn't released from his first tour until August. During his stay at home, Debbie became pregnant.

Because of a fire on the ship he was serving on, Ron's leave was extended to a year. He was there when their first child was born, a baby boy. Six months later he reported to duty for his second tour. In Viet Nam Ron guided river boats into the heart of the war. His job was to safely bring fresh troops into the battle and bring injured and deceased marines out. The boats were constantly barraged by flying bullets coming from the bushes, and frequent clouds of Agent Orange were being dropped on them. He never spoke of any of the things he had endured until the last year of his life. He did three tours in four years. He suffered from PTSD (Post Traumatic Stress Disorder) most of his life, but there was no diagnosis until 2011. As greater attention and awareness was finally coming to the forefront, he was given a disabled condition based 50% on PTSD. In 2013, he was reevaluated and they bumped it to 75% based on PTSD, with 100% unemployable status. In the meantime, Ron continued to serve his country.

During his second leave, Debbie became pregnant again. After he completed his 3rd tour he was able to be discharged, but if he left the navy at this point the birth of their baby would not be covered by his insurance. Ron remained stationed in San Diego while Debbie stayed in Phoenix for the birth of their second child. When she went into labor, her sister and mom went with her to the hospital. She was about to experience another pivotal point in her relationship with God.

The delivery was fast! The doctor didn't even make it in time, but Debbie instantly knew something was wrong. She could see that the baby was blue. She had been born in the sack, and immediately the emergency room doctor was called to break the sack and cut the cord. They rushed the baby out of the room. Debbie and Ron's baby girl was born with a hole in her heart and needed to be rushed to another hospital where there was a NICU. They brought her into Debbie to say good-bye because they didn't think she would make it through the night. She wasn't given the opportunity to touch her, so the best she could do was wave to her little one before she was whisked away.

Her mom and sister went with the baby to the hospital, Ron was still in San Diego, and Debbie was left by herself in the labor room until she could be moved to a hospital room. Alone, not knowing what was wrong with her little girl, Debbie once again cried out to God, "OK, Lord, here we are again. If you want to take her, take her. She's your child anyway. Just help Ron and me to be able to handle it. If you decide to leave her with us, help Ron and I to be the parents she needs. Either way, she's yours, she's not ours!" The same peace came over her that she had experienced many years earlier. She knew God would take care of her.

Ron was discharged the next morning with an urgent message to get home. Neither one of them knew anything at this time. Without the convenience of cell phones or Internet, Debbie's communication with everyone was very limited. When a doctor finally came in to talk with Debbie, he assumed she had been told that their baby was born with Down syndrome. Debbie didn't even know what that term meant, as it was a fairly new label. He had to explain to her that her daughter was mentally retarded and that she would probably not live past seventeen years of age. The doctor then left the room.

Shocked by the news, not having the support of loved ones around her at the moment, Debbie had no way to process everything that was happening. Debbie recalls, "But God was good." Right at that time, her pastor and her mom walked into her room. Here was one of those times when she was "hard pressed on every side, but not crushed; perplexed, but not in despair; persecuted, but not abandoned; struck down, but not destroyed" (2 Corinthians 4:8-9). God, as always, was providing a way out.

Their daughter, Little Bobbie Alaine, not only survived through the night but continues to thrive at age forty-four! She has defied the doctor's prediction! Ron and Debbie maneuvered their way through the programs and education that were available for their daughter. Debbie always thought that Bobbie was placed in their lives so that she could help others who had Down syndrome children. Those "others" were never sent her way. Over the years, and at one more pivotal point in her life, Debbie realized that she was the one who needed Bobbie.

Debbie was very involved in her church. She was teaching three classes, writing the lessons for each one, and serving on the board. When a new pastor came on board, Debbie discovered a questionable accounting issue. She reported it to the board secretary, and the board confronted the pastor. They were not questioning his intent or motivation, but the perception that could potentially get him in trouble. They wanted to help protect him. Instead he reacted in a defensive mode, and he proceeded to verbally attack Debbie in front of the rest of the board. She was left speechless, but it was God keeping her mouth shut. A praying friend in the next room was also given direction by God to leave the area, because God was in control.

Debbie and the pastor were able to resolve their issues and work together throughout the next year, but that afternoon she went home feeling devastated. She was walking and praying around the backyard when it dawned on her. The pain of rejection she was feeling gave her a glimpse of what Jesus went through when his disciples abandoned Him before the cross. The physical pain on the cross is referred to much more often than the emotional agony He experienced. She was able to thank Jesus for going through that for her!

Shortly after this revelation, her daughter, Bobbie came home from school. She was upset to see her mom crying. She slung her backpack on the floor, came up to her mom and threw her arms around her neck. She gave her a kiss on the cheek and said, "Mommy, I love you!" It hit Debbie right then and there that God knew, on that specific day, that she would need a physical kiss and words of love from Him through Bobbie.

Throughout her life, Debbie has had multiple physical trials. She was diagnosed in 1985 with Crohn's disease, an illness that was fairly unchartered at that time. There were no medications or protocols for the things she was dealing with. She had reparative surgery in 1990, and the Crohn's went into remission. In 1993 she had back surgery. She lost her husband suddenly in 2017. She is having to fight the VA for compensation of his benefits due to his PTSD, and she is actually working with the government to change policy for others who might face similar circumstances. Her Crohn's has come back with a vengeance and she is on medication to get it under control. With her husband's death, she is bearing full responsibility of caring for Bobbie. Life continues to make her weary.

Through tears of joy, Debbie came back to her life verse, Isaiah 40:28-31. The Creator God gives strength to the weary. His timing is always perfect. He provides the right people at the right time, and has prepared her for each trial and given her the peace she needed through it. Debbie doesn't want people to concentrate on all the "bad" things that have happened to her, but how God was there for her each time! She has had the opportunity to share her story with some atheists who have come into her life, acquaintances of her son's through a city softball league. They can try to deny God's existence, but they cannot deny her testimony. She is seeing some chinks in their armor. God is using her weakness to show His power and strength!

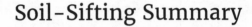

Soil-Sifting Summary

- We work hard at becoming emotionally, physically, and spiritually strong. The bottom line however, is that "...even youths grow tired and weary, and young men stumble and fall" (Isaiah 40:30).
- In order to soar like an eagle (see Isaiah 40:31), we first have to be drained and at a low point.
- We have to be weak in order to gain the power of God.
- God is good, and He provides His presence and the presence of others at just the right time and place to keep us from being overwhelmed.
- God uses our weakness to show His power and strength!

Digging into God's Word

- Isaiah 40:28-31
- 2 Corinthians 12:8-10
- 2 Corinthians 4:7-9
- Philippians 4:13

Extracting Truths and Treasures

Chapter 8

FALLING

For all have sinned and fall short of the glory of God.
Romans 3:23

$\mathcal{I}$ have had some experiences with falling. Maybe I need to pay more attention to what I'm doing instead of looking at the scenery. Last year I was walking on a paved path near the ocean. The path was gently sloping down toward a lookout spot. Instead of waiting to get to the view point, I was trying to get an early look. I didn't want to miss seeing a whale or dolphins jumping through the waves. Just as the path curved slightly to the right, my right foot caught the lip of the pavement. My ankle twisted slightly causing me to get off balance. Before I knew what was happening, I was flailing across the blacktop with no way to stop.

Falling hurts! Skinned knees and elbows sting like crazy! Bruised ribs and shins feel like they will take forever to heal. I was embarrassed, bleeding, and definitely in some pain. We were about a mile away from our hotel room, and we didn't have any first-aid materials with us. We were only taking a walk, for Pete's sake! We made our way down to the water's edge so I could wash my wounds. I was able to find a pool of water that was fairly clear of sand. The cold sea brine helped to cleanse away and slow the major blood flow. I gritted my teeth against the salt burn. I used a wadded up piece of Kleenex from my pocket to dab at the abrasions as we made our way back to our hotel.

I was sore for weeks to follow. The ensuing scars seemed to take a long time to begin to fade. They were reminders to be more careful next time!!! As fast as it took to take that spill, we experience the same dangers of slipping or falling spiritually. Sometimes it's a matter of allowing ourselves to become distracted. Other times there are obstacles in our way that cause us to trip. Still other times we let our pride get in the way, and pride comes before a fall!

My fall was fairly minor, but I truly have more empathy for young children who skin their knees on a regular basis. My friend Trina, however, had a much more serious fall. Trina is a waitress at Hodel's Country Dining in Bakersfield. It is a locally owned restaurant that serves buffet style food that is delicious and fresh every day! It has been around for 50 years, and is used frequently to cater big banquets or dinners. Our ladies' Bible study has met there at 6:00 AM, one morning a week, for about 30 years. In the last decade or so, Trina has been the server who takes care of our group. She makes sure the music is turned off in our room, our coffee cups are set and ready, and the coffee pot is full and hot. She knows who needs a diet coke and who needs their specific tea.

Trina checks in on us a couple of times, but mostly makes sure our door is closed and nobody bothers us. We check in on her occasionally to see if she has prayer requests or to see why she might have missed the previous week. Trina loves her job there, and is grateful for her Christian boss. She is a loyal employee and a dedicated worker. She is someone you can always count on.

One morning as we were gathering for our study, Trina walked in with her left hand wrapped in a towel. Even though it was obvious she had been injured, she was still determined to serve us until her replacement arrived. We got the short version of what happened, extended our concerns, and promised to pray for her. Shortly after, she was whisked to the doctor's office to get attention.

I met with Trina a few weeks later to get filled in on the details of what happened. (Warning: if you get squeamish at the thought of blood, skip the next couple of paragraphs!) As she was getting everything ready for our group, she realized she needed two more coffee cups. She walked into her work station and grabbed the cups, one in each hand. When she turned around to walk out of the station there was a little bit of water on the floor. Her foot hit the small puddled area and she fell to her knees. As a natural reflex, she put the palms of her hands out to break her fall and keep herself from face planting. Her right hand let go of the coffee cup, but her left hand kept its grip. As her hands made contact with the floor, the impact caused the coffee cup she was holding to shatter. A long shard of the broken cup was stuck into her left palm. When she held her hand up, she saw the fragment dangling from her hand.

Her automatic reaction was to pull out the piece of glass. As soon as she did, the blood came gushing out like a water hose. She got up off her knees, grabbed a towel, and put pressure on it. She immediately ran into the back where the cooks were preparing food for the day. The cooks could see she was in trouble. One of them yelled at her to raise her hand over her head. He called the owner who arrived quickly to drive Trina to the company doctor.

Even though the hour was early and before opening office hours, the doctor was on 24/7 call. The medical staff began to clean up the punctured area. They took x-rays to make sure there was no glass still in the wound. Apparently when she had pulled out the broken piece of glass she had also pulled out a chunk of skin. Because of where the opening was on the palm of her hand, the doctor would not be able to use regular stitches but would use strips of tape to close it up. Before taping it up, however, he took a pair of tweezers and was trying to push the skin back in without any numbing. Trina could feel everything! The piece of skin was not cooperating, so he decided to pull it back out and cut off the excess.

The doctor finally taped the skin together. As he was working over Trina, he said, "Right in the palm of your hand. That's kind of like Jesus." When he said that Trina immediately said, "Oh, no, you can't compare me to Jesus. What I just went through is nothing compared to what He went through for us." Trina had a new perspective. She knew how her injury felt. Yet when she thought of Jesus hanging on the cross with nails in His hands, His pain and suffering was so much greater than hers.

We had a great conversation about God's love for us. Jesus knew what was about to happen to Him, but He went through with it anyway. He endured the betrayal of friends, His arrest and false conviction by synagogue leaders, and an unfair trial before the imperial magistrate. At any point during this time He could have called down angels to rescue Him, but He continued to suffer for our ultimate salvation.

He was flogged, mocked, beaten, and spit upon. He was nailed to a cross and left to die. Even while on the cross he was taunted and scorned. It is no wonder that Jesus breathed His last breath with a loud cry. The centurion who stood by heard Jesus' cry and recognized that He didn't die in the usual way of those who are crucified. The crucified normally suffer long periods of complete agony and exhaustion, and then unconsciousness before dying. He realized that "Surely this man was the Son of God" (Mark 15:39). "But God raised him from the dead, freeing him from the agony of death, because it was impossible for death to keep its hold on him" (Acts 2:33). What Satan thought was the defeat of his foe was the path to Christ's victory. We now can participate in that victory through Christ.

Trina admitted she could not watch the movie *The Passion of the Christ*. She just can't bring herself to watch the suffering that Jesus went through for us. To think that He loves us that much is hard to comprehend. When we contemplate the reality of the love, mercy, and grace that He bestows on us, we should want to shout it from the rooftops. Trina's scar and residual tingling and pain from her accident will forever be a reminder to her of God's love for us! Hopefully we won't all have to experience physical falling, but we all have fallen short of God's glory. The good news is that we "are justified freely by his grace through the redemption that came by Christ Jesus" (Romans 3:23-24). Praise be to God!

Soil-Sifting Summary

- As fast as it takes to physically fall, we experience the same dangers of slipping or falling spiritually. Sometimes it's a matter of allowing ourselves to become distracted. Other times there are obstacles in our way that cause us to trip. Still other times we let our pride get in the way, and pride comes before a fall!
- At any point during His suffering Jesus could have called down angels to rescue Him, but He continued to suffer for our ultimate salvation.
- The Centurion realized that the way Jesus died pointed to His deity.
- What Satan thought was the defeat of his foe was the path to Christ's victory. We can now participate in that victory through Christ.
- We have all fallen short of God's glory, but are justified and redeemed by His grace!

Digging into God's Word

- Proverbs 16:18
- Matthew 26:52-54
- Mark 15:38-39
- Acts 2:22-24
- I Corinthians 15:56-57
- Romans 3:23-24

Extracting Truths and Treasures

Chapter 9

GOOD GRIEF!

Blessed are those who mourn, for they will be comforted.
Matthew 5:4

𝔗he expression "good grief!" can be a bit confusing.

The fact is that grief, which is an occasion of keen distress or sorrow, is usually not associated with anything good. We can get a better understanding of the phrase from Charlie Brown, a *Peanuts* cartoon character. For Charlie Brown the "good" of "good grief" meant large or great. It became his go-to expression when he was experiencing frustration or a large distress. He might miss kicking the football for the 100th time or crash his kite AGAIN. He would use this exclamation to express his dismay. It was his favorite way to say he was bummed out about something.

Charles Schultz, the creator of the *Peanuts* comic strips, fashioned the Charlie Brown character largely after himself. Schultz owned a smart, loyal dog. His dad was a barber, and his mom was a housewife. As a bright young boy, Schultz was allowed to skip two half elementary grades, making him the youngest in his high school class. As a result, he was a shy, timid teenager. He felt the pain of having his drawings rejected by his high school year book. Later in life, his marriage proposal to a co-worker, with whom he had fallen in love, was turned down. Charles Schultz definitely had his "good grief" moments in real life.

Biblically speaking, grief, or mourning, **is** associated with good. It's not that what we're grieving for is good, but our blessings come through the promises that we will be comforted through our time of sorrow. Jesus knew about grief. He wept over his friend Lazarus' death (see John 11:17-44). He wept as he approached Jerusalem the week before His death because they had rejected Him as God's promised Messiah (Luke 19:41-44). Jesus cried out to God in pain and agony when He was on the cross, as He bore the pain and sins of the world (see Matthew 27:45-46). He was able to endure the cross and its shame because He knew the joy that was awaiting.

That same joy is ours, knowing that we will be reunited in Heaven with those who have gone before us. We still weep and have unexpected moments of grief that sweep over us. Pastor Mark Peake said it well, "Name it sadness. Let it be sadness. It's ok to be sad." Mark is the senior pastor and head of staff at First Presbyterian Church in Monterey, California. He was speaking from experience, knowing that for no particular rhyme or reason he might have a "grief attack." He had suffered several losses in a period of a year and a half. His story resonates with anyone who has ever been effected by heartbreak and pain.

Mark was raised by parents of strong faith. They made sure their kids knew that going to church on Sunday morning was non-negotiable. Even after they had left for college, when they came back to visit on a weekend, they knew that they would be going to church. His parents both had a deep, abiding, and personal relationship with Jesus. They knew that someday their children would have to make that commitment for themselves. Going to church was not an unrealistic application of pressure. It was just their way of holding up an expectation. It's what they did as a family.

Some of Mark's earliest and fondest memories were when he was a young boy. He remembers being about three years old with his head on his mom's lap in the pew of the Riverside Baptist church. Another memory was when he would wake up in the night to get a drink of water. He would hear his parents praying together in their bedroom before they went to sleep. As they vacationed during the summer, making a trek to their grandparents' home in the South, Mark would fall asleep in the hotel room to the sound of their prayers. Their faith made a precious and indelible impression on him.

When a job change moved their family from California to Pennsylvania, they began attending a Presbyterian church. Mark's parents continued to be involved as Sunday school teachers, deacons, and elders. It was during this time of his life that he met his best friend, John. They didn't attend the same school, but they saw each other each Sunday. Almost every week, one of them would go to the others house on Sunday afternoon to hang out and play together. Mark mentioned that John was the smartest person he knew. He also displayed spiritual strength.

One day when the two young teen-age boys were hiking in the hills, they got lost. They wandered around for some time, not knowing which way to go. Fearful that they might not find their way home, they finally came across a dirt road that looked familiar. They decided to follow it, and eventually began to recognize the landmarks around them. John had them stop and thank God for helping them to find their way. Even though time and circumstances eventually separated them, Mark always kept in touch with John.

Mark's grief journey began shortly after Christmas of 2017. He received word that his mom had passed away. She had struggled with auto-immune issues all her life, but in her last year she began to fail quickly. Each day she was less lucid than the next, and with her failing mind she became more and more socially isolated. As Mark reflected on her weakening state toward the end, he also recalled her amazing strength through life.

His mom's first marriage had been an abusive situation. During an evening when her then-husband was in a drunken rage, she lay huddled in a fetal position, fearful for her own life and the lives of her children. Whether it was an angel or Jesus Himself, she was visited by someone that night. He said to her, "Be at peace!" The next morning, she gathered her things and her children and walked out safely. Her second husband died in an automobile accident when Mark was two.

Between raising a family, enduring hardship, suffering with physical issues, and suffering loss, her faith in God kept her strong. That was what was highlighted during her memorial. It was a time of worship and reflection on a life well lived. Although it was difficult, Mark was honored to officiate at her funeral.

As Christmas 2018 approached, Mark was feeling the void of his mom being gone. While celebrating at a church Christmas gathering, Mark got a call. When he looked at the number, he recognized it as John's. He had a feeling of foreboding as he calculated the difference in time on the east coast. It had to be approaching midnight, and he knew his friend wouldn't call this late unless it was important. Stepping away from the festivities, Mark was surprised that it wasn't John's voice. It was John's wife. She was sharing the devastating news that John had passed away.

After high school, John had gone down a path of addiction and eventual recovery. He married, had a family, and had a great job until he had an accident causing a traumatic brain injury. He became overwhelmed with the knowledge that he would never fully recover and never be able to work and provide for his family in the same way. He convinced himself that his family would be better off without him, so he took his own life. This was the second excruciating blow for Mark in less than a year.

The third loss came shortly after Christmas. His mom's third husband had been the dad Mark knew as he grew up. He was able to spend the last week of his dad's life with him. What a blessing it was. In spite of having Alzheimer's, his dad recognized him. Each time he saw him he would exclaim, as if happy and surprised to see him for the first time, "Hey, what are you doing here?" Each day Mark was able to spend next to his bedside, his dad was less and less responsive. On their last day together, Mark held his hand, prayed with him, and read scripture out loud. Mark was able to pour into his dad the things he knew would speak to the deepest part of his soul. The day after Mark got home, his brother called to let him know that their dad had passed away.

Three funerals is hard enough, but it was not the end. A few months after his dad's death, they had to put their sixteen-year-old dog to sleep. Mark was the one who sat next to her with his head on her heart as she breathed her last breaths. Losing a beloved pet is hard enough as it is, but in the wake of all the other loss of the past year and a half, this final loss affected him greatly. God's grace was manifested in an unexpected way during these moments as the veterinarian sensed his grief, let him cry, and hugged him in true empathy and sympathy.

How do you land on **solid ground** after a series of events like these? Mark landed on God's Word. Sure, he's a pastor, and he's supposed to go to the Bible and its promises. For Mark, though, it was more than a profession or an obligation. It was a deep and abiding faith and trust that kept him going. He claimed Jesus' words, "Do not let your hearts be troubled" (John 14:1a). He felt these words were whispered to him specifically as more than a comfort, but as a command. Beyond his true and abiding hope of being unified with his loved ones someday, he felt like he could be at peace simply because God was telling him to be at peace. He continued to lean on God and worship Him because He was God. We like receiving blessings. We may fear hell or cling to the anticipation of eternal life, but ultimately we must come to a place where we know that God is sovereign. He is in control. He has done everything that needs to be done so that we can have a relationship with Jesus. That is enough!

To illustrate this thought, Mark told how the night before his wife had gone to pick up their oldest son at a friend's house. Mark was with their younger son, Jonah. Jonah began to hear voices floating in from the backyard, most likely a close neighbor's outdoor gathering. He expressed his fear that someone was in their back yard. Mark assured him that everything was alright. He then invited him to crawl in bed with him. Jonah crawled under the covers and put his head in the crook of his dad's arm. There was nothing else that needed to be done. Dad didn't need to get a flashlight, check under the bed, or close the closet. It was enough just to hear the words, "It's ok."

It's like that with God. We don't need to fret and worry. He will shield us and hold us. He will let us be sad. He will give us peace and eventual joy. We just have to let God be God and rest in His arms. He will bless us when we mourn. He will show us "good grief."

Soil-Sifting Summary

- It's not that what we're grieving for is good, but our blessings come through the promises that we will be comforted through our time of sorrow.
- He was able to endure the cross and its shame because He knew the joy that was awaiting.
- The active, lived-out faith of parents make precious and indelible impressions on their children.
- "Do not be afraid," is not just a comfort, it is a command to help us understand the sovereignty of God.
- We don't need to fret and worry. God will shield us and hold us. He will let us be sad. He will give us peace and eventual joy. We just have to let God be God and rest in His arms.

Digging into God's Word

- Matthew 5:4
- Hebrews 12:2
- Deuteronomy 11:18-21
- John 14:27
- Deuteronomy 33:12

Extracting Truths and Treasures

Chapter 10

DO YOU BELIEVE IN MIRACLES?

The weapons we fight with are not the weapons of the world. On the contrary, they have divine power to demolish strongholds.
2 Corinthians 10:4

In the 1980 Winter Olympics, the USA hockey team was set to compete in Lake Placid, New York. The team was the youngest in the tournament and in U.S. national team history. They consisted exclusively of amateur players, but somehow made their way up the ranks to the Olympic semifinals. Their first opponent in the medal rounds was the Soviet team, who in contrast consisted primarily of professional players with significant international experience. The Soviet Union had won five of the six previous Winter Olympic Games, and they were the favorites to win the gold again this year.

In a back and forth battle, the U.S. team took their first lead in the 3rd and final period. They held on to win the game in a 4 to 3 victory. As the final seconds of the game approached ABC's Al Michaels declared, "Do you believe in miracles? YES!" The "Miracle on Ice" team went on to clinch the gold medal by beating Sweden in the final game.

As iconic as this event was, and as competitive as I can be, it doesn't even hold a candle to baby Luna's miracle. This story starts with a song. Every once in a while a song will come out that is especially anointed. Released in digital form on March 8, 2019, "Raise a Hallelujah" was written by Jake Stevens, Jonathan David Helser, Melissa Helser and Molly Skaggs of Bethel Music. It was in response to a life-threatening situation that a little boy, the son of their chief executive officer, was facing. As the song was played over and over again in the hospital room, the little one began improving. He eventually made a full recovery. The words of the chorus go like this:

> I raise a hallelujah, in the presence of my enemies
> I raise a hallelujah, louder than the unbelief
> I raise a hallelujah, my weapon is a melody
> I raise a hallelujah, heaven comes to fight for me

The phrase, "my weapon is a melody," is a picture of Brian and Hannah Tolley. They are a young couple with two children, ages one and two. Brian and Hannah lead music at their church in Santa Paula, California. On the last weekend in March of 2019, they left their two little ones with Hannah's mom so they could facilitate worship at a ladies' retreat in Cambria, just up the coast a few hours.

On Sunday, March 31, as they were beginning their way home, Hannah's mom called to let them know that baby Luna, then nine months, was running a fever and seemed a little out of sorts. It didn't seem too out of the ordinary since Luna had been teething, but they promised to keep in touch. They stopped for lunch in the Pismo area. Grandma called again to say she was putting Luna down for an early nap. She had thrown up, and grandma was going to sit by her crib to keep an eye on her. There was still no major concern. They figured she might have caught some type of "bug."

Grabbing a cup of coffee in Santa Barbara, continuing to enjoy the last few moments together without kids, Hannah and Brian received a final call. This time, Hannah's mom expressed grave concern. Luna had thrown up a few more times in bed. Now her foot was uncontrollably twitching. It was evident she needed to be taken to the emergency room.

Brian and Hannah had only one focus at this point: to get to the hospital as soon as possible. They arrived to see Luna, a normally vibrant and active infant, in a hospital bed. She was still, lethargic, and silently crying. The left side of her face appeared to be slightly drooped, and Hannah's first reaction was one of panic.

When the doctor finally called them in to go over the CT scan and X-ray results, he told them that she had severe bleeding and swelling of the brain that could only have happened with acute trauma—being dropped, hit, or shaken. The Sherriff and CPS arrived shortly after the doctor's assessment to begin questioning grandma and others involved. Hannah's mom was beside herself. Knowing that nothing like that had happened, she found herself telling and retelling the sequence of events over and over.

In the meantime, Luna was strapped to a board to prevent further damage, and ambulance transportation from Santa Paula to Children's Hospital in Los Angeles (CHLA) was dispatched. Even during this initial nightmare of events, Brian and Hannah could see God's hand. Though they were shaken to their core and feeling the **solid ground** beneath their feet give way, they knew God was not shaken and His compassion covered them.

First of all, they had just come from an amazing weekend where they had drawn closer to God and each other. Singing with these women had been life-giving and rejuvenating. The next of many God-moments occurred when the ambulance arrived. The driver was a friend of Brian's from his days as an EMT. Normally only one parent is allowed to ride with their child, but because of the connection, permission was granted for both parents to travel with her. Hannah couldn't hold her daughter who was listlessly tied to the hard surface of the board, but she could sing and pray over her.

The theme song of the weekend had been the newly released "Raise a Hallelujah." Fresh on their hearts and minds, Brian and Hannah began to claim a miracle for this precious one. They posted the situation on Facebook in order to gather prayer warriors to begin fighting the strongholds of whatever disease or ailment had attacked little Luna. Hannah's message was loud and clear as she typed in bold capital letters, **"GOD HAS HER!"**

As soon as they arrived at CHLA the brain surgeon looked at Luna's films that had been sent with her. He declared that the brain damage was from old trauma, and Hannah's mom was instantly recused. Luna was immediately taken off the board. Though there were no answers yet, Hannah was able to hold her baby for the first time since they had been reunited. As she continued to pray and sing over her, a nurse walked into their room. She recognized the song Hannah was singing and told them she would be praying for them. It was their first hospital contact. It was not the nurse who had been assigned to them, and they never saw that particular nurse again. It was in these small moments that Hannah and Brian were uplifted and affirmed in their faith.

Luna was transferred to the Pediatric Intensive Care Unit (PICU). As tests and multiple blood draws were performed on the tiny veins, the news kept getting worse. After signing papers to put

Luna under anesthesia and have her intubated, not knowing if she would wake again, Luna began a day of tests including an MRI, MRV, MRA and spinal tap. The results showed that she had experienced a stroke which had caused severe brain damage. There was no indication as to what had caused the stroke or whether she would ever be back to normal. Hannah remembers simply falling to the floor and sobbing as she heard these words.

The next few days were a waiting game. Luna began to have seizures. She remained on antibiotics in case there was an infection that was the culprit, but all the tests were coming back negative. Through the ups and downs of these difficult days, God kept showing up in small sweet ways. A friend showed up with blankets, pillows, food, toothpaste, deodorant, and a brush. The young couple had not been able to even think about taking care of themselves, and here was someone ministering to them in a tangible way. Through the Facebook posts, they began receiving word that hundreds, if not thousands, of people were praying all over the world. There were people praying in New York, Paris, Ethiopia, and Chile. When God's people unite in prayer, the power of God is present.

A couple of celebrities began to follow the story, and one sent Hannah words of encouragement and support. The town of Santa Paula united with banners around town, purple ribbons tied to light posts and fences, and fundraising support to help them with expenses that were looming. One person made and sold leather bracelets and another sold candles. The local tattoo shop gave a day's proceeds, raising over $6000. There was a line down the block throughout the day as people waited from 10 AM to 1 AM for their body art. The owners finally had to close because they had run out of ink. Every day Brian and Hannah's Venmo and GoFundMe accounts would receive donations. Brian and Hannah were blown away and humbled!

Brian and Hannah wanted to live out their faith well, knowing that so many were watching. They let their supporters know that they had surrendered Luna's entire body to God. No matter the outcome, their faith in God would not waver. God was their strength throughout. When Hannah was overcome with fear, Brian seemed to be able to hold her up. When Brian would be falling apart, Hannah would be the resilient one. When they both seemed at the bottom, friends and family would be there to pray with them as pillars of God's strength.

After a second series of tests, Brian and Hannah were called into a small room with the heads of all the departments and teams that were working on Luna's case. They knew something must be serious as they walked in to hear the latest prognosis. The word that kept coming up was "devastating." Her brain damage was so destructive, they expected her to only recover five to ten percent of her normal functions. She might not be able to swallow, eat, blink, walk, talk, or respond to her parents. They were basically saying she could very likely be a vegetable the rest of her life.

Brian and Hannah could not believe what they were hearing. They continued to seek prayer and trust God for whatever their future might hold. God said, "Watch this!" By the next day Luna's eyes were open, and she was tracking her parents. She was sucking on her pacifier and a swallow test was done giving Hannah the go-ahead to nurse. With no further seizures and a stabilization of vitals, Luna was moved down to a regular floor. That night, she began to raise her left arm. Hannah and her sister were dancing and rejoicing, only to find out the next morning that the movements that were coming at frequent intervals were more seizures.

Brian and Hannah stood over Luna's bed waiting to be transferred back to PICU. Their eyes were filled with tears, and they were feeling defeated. A team of six doctors had entered the room, and for the moment everyone was quiet. Out of the silence, the head doctor asked, "Would it be helpful if I prayed?" Hannah couldn't even answer, but she grabbed the doctor's hand and started crying harder. The sweet presence of Jesus was brought down into this hospital room by a virtual stranger who called on the name of the One who knew and loved this family and this little baby. The God of miracles was their only hope at this point!

Continuing to be perplexed by Luna's case, several possible procedures were discussed, but in the ensuing days, Luna once again began to show signs of slow progress. By day seven, the neurologist was seeing improved left side function and was hopeful that over time and with therapy Luna would make huge strides. Back in the PICU, Luna took a turn for the good. Though their hearts were breaking when Luna had to return to intensive care, Hannah could see God's hand even in this event. In the PICU there was one-on-one care and closer monitoring. They began having daily meetings with Luna's medical team to determine the steps for that day. She began to smile, pulled on her feeding tube until it came out, said "dada," and used her right hand to wave and hold a toy. She was eating on her own and continuing to fight!

After two weeks, Luna was taken out of isolation and got to see her big brother. She started physical therapy, which was a miracle in itself. The therapists said that children this young can't tolerate therapy, but somehow Luna qualified. For three hours a day she cooperated with a speech therapist, an occupational therapist, and a physical therapist. They were amazed at how motivated Luna was. She wanted to play! She worked hard at using her left hand! She was the favorite among the rehab patients.

Luna remained in the hospital for rehabilitation for an additional four weeks. The doctors never did find a reason for her initial problems. Without a cause, they couldn't prescribe a solution. The only thing that could account for her progress was a miracle. Doctor after doctor, some hesitantly, agreed that Luna's recovery was a super-natural wonder, and Brian and Hannah gave glory to God.

Throughout the tough months of waiting and watching, Brian and Hannah were in awe at God's faithfulness. The number of people praying, from motorcycle riders to little old ladies, was mind-boggling. People were touched by Luna's story, and those who followed her or who are reading about her today will never be the same. The Tolleys received messages from people who said their faith in God had been restored. Others said they were revisiting church and starting to pray again. As the body of Christ unified in prayer over this family, God's power and majesty were revealed over and over again. Brian and Hannah recognized that what had happened to their little family was being used to advance the gospel.

Luna is home today. She continues getting weekly therapy, and she is improving each day. Her potential five percent recovery is much closer to ninety percent. She is sitting up, crawling, chattering, smiling, voluntarily using her left side, and defying all odds that were against her. Do you believe in miracles? Luna's name literally means moon. Her miracle will always be a light that shines in the darkness.

Soil-Sifting Summary

- I raise a hallelujah, in the presence of my enemies

  I raise a hallelujah, louder than the unbelief

  I raise a hallelujah, my weapon is a melody

  I raise a hallelujah, heaven comes to fight for me
- Though we are shaken to our core and feel the **solid ground** beneath our feet give way, God is not shaken and His compassion covers us.
- When God's people unite in prayer, the power of God is present.
- No matter the outcome, God remains our strength.
- The trials that happen to us can be used to advance the gospel.
- May our lives be like Luna's miracle—lights that shine in the darkness.

Digging into God's Word

- 2 Corinthians 10:3-5
- Isaiah 54:10
- Matthew 18:19-20
- Habakkuk 3:17-19
- Philippians 1:12-14
- Matthew 5:14-16

Extracting Truths and Treasures

Christ,
Our Sure and Steadfast
Path

Chapter 11

LEVEL GROUND

Teach me to do your will, for you are my God; may your good Spirit lead me on level ground. Psalm 143:10

We all dread the "C" word, "Cancer." If there is anything that can make us feel like we are slipping into an abyss, it is hearing the doctor say a biopsy is needed to check for potential malignancy. The information we can garner on the Internet is both a blessing and a curse. On the one hand, we don't have to wait for some of our questions to be answered. On the other hand, we can read about the worst possible outcomes, and our minds tend to dwell in a place of fear. Whether the patient is you or someone you love, it is difficult to think positively.

We received word from my mom in late January 2019 that my cousin had a mass on her ovary that was suspicious. They were looking into where and how they could get the most timely and expert care in order to get more definitive answers. My Bible study group began to immediately pray, as did groups of family and friends across the United States. People they knew in Japan, where Sandy and her husband had lived for almost 9 years, also started a prayer chain. The family of God is amazing when it comes to prayer!

We all had questions. When did all this begin? Sandy started noticing something not feeling right in her abdomen shortly before Thanksgiving, 2018. It really didn't hurt, and she had experienced a similar pulling sensation with previous fibroids. With company coming in a few days, Sandy didn't feel a real urgency to do anything immediately. She kept putting it off, not being fond of doctor appointments. In December as she was with her dad, who was in the hospital with heart issues, she felt the prompting of the Holy Spirit that she should get this issue checked out.

When Sandy tried to make an appointment, she discovered that since it had been so long since she had been to her doctor, she had to establish herself as a new patient. Weeks went by before she could get the January exam scheduled. Almost as soon as the check-up began the doctor said, "Oh, I feel a mass." This kicked into gear a series of additional assessments that were needed. Sandy needed blood work, and her husband, Craig, made her do it the next day. She needed a CT scan, which again couldn't be scheduled for a couple of weeks.

She finally had the scan done on a Monday. The very next morning, less than 24 hours later, the doctor's phone number appeared in Sandy's phone. She immediately began to feel a sense of foreboding and fear. The results showed it was definitely a mass on her ovary and it was suspicious for ovarian cancer. Her doctor went on to say she had already scheduled an appointment with the local oncologist on Thursday and had arranged for an appointment with the City of Hope. Sandy was thinking, "You don't get a referral to the City of Hope unless they think you have cancer." Thursday morning the local oncologist's office called and told Sandy that he didn't see any point in seeing her. She just needed to go straight to the City of Hope. Her fears increased.

Sandy was assigned to a "nurse navigator." She was actually able to get the appointment at City of Hope a week earlier than had originally been scheduled, but still about 3 weeks away. She was also referred to UCLA Medical Center. It would be good to get a second opinion and UCLA might have an earlier opening. As they were talking, Sandy said, "So...we're calling this cancer?" The nurse navigator replied, "Yes." Now her fears were turning to panic.

UCLA called that night with an automated service that told Sandy what to do to get the ball rolling with them. Her phone call to UCLA the next morning lasted about 30 minutes, as they were getting information about Sandy into their system. At one point Sandy was going to be put on hold. She expressed concern that they might get cut off. The reply came back, "Don't worry, I won't lose you!" Those words were just what Sandy needed at that moment, helping her feel confident in the UCLA process and staff. Once her patient account was established, she was given the names and phone numbers of two doctors. She chose one and called to make an appointment. This choice was definitely ordained by God. Looking back, Sandy knew that God was leading her. The doctor could see her on February 19, again three to four weeks away. She was thinking, "I have cancer, yet I can't get in to see someone!"

Sandy's friend, Kim, was one of the first people Sandy spoke to about her diagnosis. Kim had walked through a battle the previous year with breast cancer. She advised Sandy to not assume the worst (easier said than done). She told her that they didn't KNOW if it was cancer. Sandy received the same word from her sister-in-law and from a family friend who was a nurse in San Diego. Kim also told her that when she called for her appointments, she should always ask to be put on call in case of a cancellation or ask if there would be any way to get in faster. Sandy did that, and the person in the office said she would text the doctor.

The very next morning, a Friday, Sandy's office manager, a woman of great faith, approached her. She shared how she had been praying for her the previous night. Sandy told her of the scripture she had been claiming that says, "Let the morning bring me word of your unfailing love, for I have put my trust in you. Show me the way I should go, for to you I lift up my soul. (Psalm 143:8)" While they were talking, UCLA called and asked if Sandy could come in the next Monday, February 4. The scripture promise was being fulfilled right in front of them both!

Sandy made a reservation at the UCLA guest house for Sunday night, so they wouldn't have to stress about traffic on Monday. On Monday morning Sandy noticed in the room on the counter there was a little complementary lotion that was called "Peace be Still." It was another word from the Lord in the morning, reminding her of His unfailing love. So many words of encouragement, many from things she read, came in the morning. Sandy reflected on how she has always had her quiet devotional time with the Lord in the morning. She admonished us all to make sure we make ourselves available to hear what the Lord wants to teach us for the day.

As Sandy was preparing to go to that first UCLA appointment, she was praying, yet had so much fear in her heart. God gave her the overwhelming sense that Jesus was there, walking the halls of the hospital. He knew what was going on behind each of those doors, and He knew what was going on with Sandy. It provided such a comfort for her. She was learning, through her fears, that God loves HER! She always felt like she knew God loved everybody else, but never felt like she was deserving of His love. Psalm 143:2 talks about how no one living is righteous before God. It is true that we don't deserve His goodness. That's what makes His love for us and His faithfulness to us that much more amazing! This journey with God enabled Sandy to get past her feelings of unworthiness. She sensed His love at every turn and was embracing this acceptance and value from Him.

The doctor talked to Sandy and Craig first, setting them at ease. As the exam proceeded, she said, "Oh, it's moving around, that's a good sign. It's big, about the size of a volleyball." At the conclusion, the doctor's first words were that it could be benign. Sandy and Craig were clinging to that hope! Other possibilities were that it could be cancer, or it could be a border-line situation. Regardless, surgery needed to be scheduled. The earliest date they could book was March 4, a month away!

If Sandy ever had any doubts about God directing her steps, those were dispelled when she met Dr. Memarzadeh, the gynecological oncologist, for the first time. She had a team of about six doctors, from interns to fellows, all following her every step, wanting to be just like her. She coached, mentored, and taught these doctors, and they had nothing but good things to say about her. When Sandy expressed that the surgery date seemed to be so far off—"Don't I need this to happen as soon as possible?"—Dr. Memarzadeh assured her that the time frame for getting ready for surgery was reasonable. Once again there was confirmation and peace. It ended up taking the better part of the month to get all the appointments taken care of on the action list.

With a surgery date reserved, and a list of action items to be done before surgery day, they got right to it. The first item on the agenda was to get more blood drawn. Sandy panicked a bit when she saw the number of vials that would have to be drawn, but the phlebotomist kept her distracted and did a good job. The next thing she had to do was get medically approved by her doctor at home.

This meant checking her out more thoroughly and running more tests to make sure she was surgery-ready. Again, she was having a hard time getting a timely appointment. She was concerned that she wouldn't get her approval for surgery in time, but even that worked out. They were able to bump her up to a suitable date.

Another one of the action items was to get a mammogram. Sandy got a call back from the imaging service, saying that they had seen abnormal shadows in the pictures. Again, with fear and trembling, Sandy, accompanied by Craig, got to her call back appointment about 45 minutes early. She went ahead and checked in and was taken back within 5 minutes. Shortly after the procedures were completed both the radiologist and the tech came back to assure them that she was clear! All of that happened by the time her appointment should have begun. Craig and Sandy were able to leave rejoicing and relieved that there was one less thing to worry about!

At one point Sandy became conflicted about whether or not to get a second opinion at City of Hope. Again, God gave her a peace about where He had sent her. She had nothing but good things to say about how the UCLA team treated and cared for her. They were so thoughtful. They would do things without her even asking, like making sure she could get her radiology and CT scan appointments on the same day so she wouldn't have to make two trips.

Even though the mammogram had been done, UCLA wanted to do a follow up. Sandy felt like it was a little bit of over-kill since she had already been cleared, but the doctor wanted a second look. The technician confirmed that all breast issues were benign. The technician shared that her own hysterectomy had been done by Dr. Memarzadeh because there was ovarian cancer in her family line.

She told Sandy how great the doctor was, and that after her surgery she was back to work in 4 days. The second test may not have been necessary, but God knew the conversation with the tech would be another confirmation that she was in good care.

The night before surgery day, they were joined by three couples: their son and his wife, Sandy's brother and his wife, and her friend Kim and her husband. They had a pre-surgery dinner "party" at a Vietnamese restaurant. It helped keep Sandy distracted. It was good to laugh! The next morning Sandy arrived at the hospital to find they were behind and not ready for her to begin the pre-op preparations. This didn't help in the anxiety department, but being able to continue the visit with friends and family helped the time pass.

Finally, they began prepping her. The anesthesiologist was talking about giving Sandy an epidural. This was the first she had heard about it, and she was questioning the purpose behind needing this procedure. At that moment, her doctor walked in, listened to Sandy's concern, and simply stated that she had done hundreds of these operations **without** an epidural. Relieved that her doctor had performed many successful surgeries similar to hers and was in total control of the situation, Sandy slipped into her medicine-induced dreamland.

The next thing she knew she was waking up. The first words out of Craig's mouth were, "You don't have cancer!" Sandy kept saying it was the best day of her life. She had great post-op care in a transitional care unit. They were at her beck and call. Her pain was way more minimal than she had expected. Within a few days, she was being released to go home and continue the healing process.

As Sandy was sharing her story over lunch, we stopped to thank God for His goodness. All along the way, there were so many decisions! It was new territory, and Sandy had to seek God. Many times she felt a clear direction. God was teaching her His will as He led her to the right hospital, the right surgeon, the right appointments, the right words of encouragement—all at the right time. His good Spirit was leading her along **solid** and level **ground**.

 ## Soil-Sifting Summary

- As we lift our hearts and praise to God in the mornings, He honors our trust in Him with affirmations of His unfailing love.
- We need to make sure we make ourselves available each morning to hear what the Lord wants to teach us for the day.
- God loves us! He sometimes uses our trials and fears to bring us to a place where we can see His love, guidance, comfort, and direction at every turn.
- When we are in new territory, we have to seek God. Many times we feel a clear direction. God teaches us His will. His good Spirit leads us along solid and level ground.

Digging into God's Word

- Psalm 143:8
- Lamentations 3:22-25
- Jeremiah 31:3-4
- Psalm 143:10

Extracting Truths and Treasures

Chapter 12

MAP MY WALK

Blessed are all who fear the Lord, who walks in his ways.
Psalm 128:1

There are a lot of technology companies these days that claim to motivate you to reach your health and fitness goals by tracking your activity, exercise, sleep, weight, and more. Their device or app promises to measure your steps, your heart rate, and your quality of sleep. When I inquired of Richard what he used when he trained, he told me he uses an app on his phone called MapMyWalk. This was such a perfect name for tracking Richard's power walking ventures. He wanted God to map his way and guide him through his training and competitions.

Richard Newton has always loved to walk...and walk FAST! Once when he and his wife were at the mall, he was walking and talking with her. He got quite a ways down the corridor when he realized that the woman he was talking to was not his wife. He apologized to this stranger, who was quite tickled at what had just transpired. Looking back toward the way he had come, he saw his wife several stores away, smiling and waving. She had decided she couldn't keep up with him, and she reasoned that he would figure out soon enough that she wasn't beside him.

Richard deduc:ed that he was just a fast walker. He decided one day to do something with that revelation. One night while getting ready for bed, he told his wife that he was going to get up early the next morning and walk around the block. He timed the three-mile route and kept this routine for thirty-one days straight. Each day he would try to beat "yesterday's" time. He improved his time from thirty-two minutes to twenty-five minutes!

Richard continued to increase his distance from three, to four, to five, to six miles. His sister-in-law introduced him to the MapMyWalk app that would keep track of his miles, his calories, his route, and his time, right from his phone. Richard was thrilled with the information and began to use it immediately.

At church one Sunday, Team World Vision introduced its marathon that raises money for providing clean water and fullness of life for families in Africa. Richard decided he would try it. He worked with the team to train, but he felt like there was something missing. The next time the team met he prayed, "God, just meet me where I'm at." He began calling out to God while he was walking. This began his journey of praying while he walked. He kept seeking God, asking Him to reveal His strength and His plan. He was asking God to map his walk.

God made it clear to Richard that He wanted him to pray for whoever was in front of him while he walked. Richard's lightbulb turned on. He started to pray for the other walkers and bike riders on the trail. He prayed for their safety, for an outpouring of God's grace on them, and for God to meet them where they were. It was simple. Richard was obedient.

Then God said, "Do more. Call them by name." Since Richard didn't know their names, he began to greet each person with a good morning and a smile. No one responded back. There wasn't even a head nod. It was more like they were just wanting him to get out of their way.

God promises that if we walk in His ways and perform His service, He will bless us and grant us free access to those who are standing (or in this case, walking) there (see Zechariah 3:7) Richard kept being obedient to what he felt God was calling him to do. One ten-mile training day, things began to change. He said, "Hi," to a gentleman who was coming in the other direction. He got a response! They engaged in conversation about his camo pack. Richard found out his name, and a friendship started that day.

That inspired Richard all the more to talk to people, but he was still concerned about improving and working on his time. One morning he did a nine-mile walk. When he got to his turn-around point, there was a homeless man walking by. God told Richard to give him some water. Richard argued that this was the only water he had and he might need it on the return nine miles. The message from God was clear, so Richard approached the man and asked if he could use some water. The man graciously accepted saying he was so thirsty! They talked for about five minutes, and Richard said a prayer over him.

Concerned about his strength and lack of water for the return miles, Richard asked God to help him get back to his car. He was also a little frustrated that doing "God's work" was going to affect his time. As his phone started talking to him, he was shocked to realize that the brief interlude had not affected his time at all. It occurred to Richard that God creates time for us to do his work. He is not limited to time and space as we know it. We think we are too busy, but when we are obedient, God creates the extra minutes we need.

With his training complete, the day of Richard's first marathon came. Richard had teamed up with another runner named Allen. As Richard was completing the first half, Satan started playing tricks on his mind and he didn't think he could finish. He prayed for God to give him the strength that he needed, and he just kept putting one foot in front of the other until he reached his partner. Later on he got a text from Allen that their combined time was better than anyone else from their team. Allen told Richard he had rocked his half, and that he had even come in at a faster time than Allen. Richard was amazed, and gave God the glory.

Now he had a new goal—to give God the glory after each mile was accomplished. "To you be the glory for that last mile. I praise your name! Go before me this next mile. Clear my path of any obstacles. Keep me upright. Don't let me stumble and fall. Let my path cross with somebody you want me to talk to." He was power walking on the **solid ground** of Jesus, and it changed Richard's perspective.

Richard got inspired to start training for full marathons and entered his first one in Bakersfield. He asked God how he could honor Him. He decided to have his bib say "Walking 4 Jesus." Race day came. Richard was nervous, but he was prepared and excited. The announcer looked dubiously at his shirt and was even more doubtful that Richard would be able to finish. Richard knew he couldn't hide from the truth that was printed on his back. He prayed that he would not appear arrogant or self-righteous, but that he could be a witness for Jesus.

Richard was on a mission. He prayed for those he passed and for those who passed him. As the race ensued, he had an opportunity to cheer on a runner who was really struggling. Richard just encouraged him and pushed him to keep going. Soon they reached the crest of the hill and off the runner went. Richard breathed a prayer of thanks and safety for the runner. Somehow much further down the route, Richard caught up with him again. The runner was really laboring, even though the end of the race was getting close. Richard told him that he felt that God asked him to stay with him. They had an amazing conversation. As they turned the corner, they could see the finish line. Richard told the guy to go ahead of him and wait for him on the other side of the finish line.

In our walk with God, there will be those who go before us and cross the Finish Line of life. This cloud of witnesses will be waiting for us on the other side urging us on. As Richard came through, his new friend was applauding and backing Richard's strong completion of the race. The announcer began to proclaim the name on his bib, "And here comes Richard, 'Walking...For...Jesus!'" His face registered a bit of shock and a lot of respect. Richard's walk had matched his talk. He was ministering to so many around him, and they could see his good deeds were in line with the Good Word across his shoulders.

As Richard continued to enter marathons, he always included "Walking 4 Jesus" after his name on the back of his shirt. He knew everyone going by would see it, whether they liked it or not. He asked God to protect his back and to bless those who would be against it and those who would be for it. When anyone asked him about it, Richard just replied that he couldn't do it without God. God had brought him this far, and he was trusting God to help him finish.

Richard and his shirt continued to witness to people. The next year he added "I'm praying for you!" on the back of his shirt.

Richard liked staying in the middle of the road to avoid the slight sloping on the street toward the curb, which bothered his ankles. In one particular race, as he was going along down the middle of the road, he felt like God was telling him to walk on the side. He drifted to the left, and immediately people began thanking him for his prayers. He went back to the middle, and there was nothing. He drifted to the right, and again he heard people thanking him and asking him to pray that they finish the race. It dawned on him that God knew where the people were who needed him. He trusted God to strengthen his ankles. He received more thanks and gratitude than ever before. As he followed the path God was mapping out for him, he was being blessed and was blessing others.

The climate began changing on his daily walks as well. He inspired a group of bicyclists to print "Bikers 4 Jesus" on their shirts. He was getting so many opportunities to share Jesus! People always asked what his shirt was all about. He was happy to tell them, "I'm unable on my own." He counted on God to get him through his walking each day.

God also used Richard's walking to help him grow personally and spiritually. One particular time Richard was questioning his purpose at work. He wondered if maybe it was time to move on. Frustrated and venting, he was seeking a word from the Lord. As Richard walked, God asked him, "Do you truly love me?" When Richard was truly honest with himself, he answered, "God, I do love you, but I can't say I truly love you right now. My heart's not in the right place." He was crying his eyes out as he confessed his shortcomings before the Lord and let the Holy Spirit begin transforming his own spirit. Concerned runners were stopping to ask him if he was alright. Richard said, "I've never been better. Do you know how the Holy Spirit works? He's working in me. I'm good."

In tough times Richard has learned to rebuke Satan and call on the name of Jesus. As soon as he mentions the name of Jesus, he senses the Spirit bringing him joy and love, power and grace. God literally maps his walk. One fall day Richard, who was now used to doing an average of fourteen miles, was struggling at mile three. His feet felt like they had weights on them. He was literally dragging his feet through the piles of leaves wondering if there was something physically wrong with him. He decided he should get back to his car before he had to call someone to come and rescue him.

He called on the Lord, asking Him to lead him, keep him from obstacles ahead, direct him to those who needed a touch from God. The minute he turned around, the feeling of weights lifted. Almost immediately he ran into a couple of members of the team who needed prayer. Another and then another crossed his path who needed a word from the Lord or prayer. He got back to the park and was feeling great so he headed back out. The same thing happened three times, struggling in one direction, encountering needs when he turned around. He was now at eighteen miles, and God let him know he was done for the day. "Obedience is the key," Richard said as we concluded our interview. His journey and example is an encouragement to us to let God map our way and lead us to walk before Him in the light of life.

Soil-Sifting Summary

- God promises that if we walk in His ways and perform His service, He will bless us and grant us free access to those who are standing there.
- God creates time for us to do his work. He is not limited to time and space as we know it. We think we are too busy, but when we are obedient God creates the extra minutes we need.
- In our walk with God, there will be those who go before us and cross the Finish Line of life. This cloud of witnesses will be waiting for us on the other side urging us on.
- Richard's walk had matched his talk. He was ministering to so many around him as they could see his good deeds were in line with the Good Word across his shoulders.
- God knows where the people are who need Him. We must trust God to strengthen us wherever He takes us. As we follow the path God maps out for us, we will be blessed and be a blessing to others.
- Let God map your way and lead you to walk before Him in the light of life.

Digging into God's Word

- Zechariah 3:7
- 2 Peter 3:8-9
- Hebrews 12:1
- 2 Thessalonians 2:16-17
- Psalm 128:1
- Psalm 56:13

Extracting Truths and Treasures

_____

_____
_____
_____
_____
_____
_____
_____
_____
_____
_____
_____
_____
_____
_____
_____
_____
_____
_____
_____
_____
_____
_____
_____
_____
_____
_____
_____
_____
_____
_____

Chapter 13

VICTORIOUS ONE

I press on toward the goal to win the prize for which God has called me heavenward in Christ Jesus. Philippians 3:14

$\mathcal{I}$ absolutely love the book of Philippians. From the time I was a young teen I can remember finding spiritual nuggets from this book that have helped me live out my Christian life. As student chaplain of my college women's choir, I developed a Bible study for our spring tour. I called it "Phinding Phood in Philippians." I have passages underlined and notes all over the margins of Philippians in my Bible. It is a precious volume to me. Even today, I go back to this book often for reminders of what attitudes I should have toward others and circumstances. It is a foundational place for me to land, my **solid ground**.

As an elementary school teacher, it somehow bothered me when in the 70s and 80s there was such a strong emphasis on building students' self-esteem. I wasn't quite sure why this disturbed me at first. Students **need** to feel confident about their abilities and uniqueness. I came to realize that what concerned me was the emphasis of believing in and honoring self. Our esteem does not come from within ourselves, but through Christ. Philippians 1:6 made it clear that what was needed was not **self**-esteem, but **Christ**-esteem, confidence that "...he who began a good work in you will carry it on to completion..."

The second chapter of Philippians has been particularly meaningful. It is a call to love others, putting their interests before your own. This applies to relationships at work, within the body of believers, in marriage, and with family. Christ modeled this humility to the point of His death on the cross. "He did not consider equality with God something to be grasped" (Philippians 2:6). Our problem is we want to be equal with God. Jesus **is** God's equal, yet he humbled himself. You and I will never be God's equal, yet we try to play god in our own lives. If you're like me, you've learned that doesn't work. His way of servanthood and obedience does work.

Then Paul gives a visual description of what it will be like when every knee will bow and every tongue confess that Jesus Christ is Lord, to the glory of God the Father (see Philippians 2:9-11). Can you see it? People from every tribe and nation, speaking every language ever spoken on this earth, will be exalting Jesus as Lord. His very presence will cause us all to drop to our knees in honor of the One and Only King of Kings and Lord of Lords. It sends chills down my spine as I rejoice in the scene of Christians everywhere recognizing their Savior. It saddens me as I think of those who will not enter His Kingdom because they have rejected Him.

That's why we need to "shine like stars in the universe" as we live amongst "a crooked and depraved generation"(see Philippians 2:15). There are so many who are destitute for Him. There are so many who are in our sphere of influence who are crying out to hear the Good News. We are called to share the joy that can be experienced by all who lay their sin at His feet and confess that Jesus is Lord.

Too often we have excuses as to why we can't or don't share Jesus' love with others. It usually has to do with our lack of confidence and our knowledge of our character flaws. I have come to strongly believe that every character quality we have has been given to us by the Lord. He wishes to use it for good, but Satan wants to twist it for evil. Take Saul of Tarsus (aka Paul), the writer of Philippians, for example. He was passionate about a cause, just the wrong one. He was out to imprison all Christians. He was very efficient in what he did. He went right to the top. He got letters from the high priest to arrest any worshipers in the synagogues who belonged to "The Way."

As Saul continued his zealous mission, he was stopped on the road to Damascus. Jesus met him and in essence said, "You are being passionate about the wrong things. I know you, I created you and every aspect of your personality. Now, shut your eyes to the things you think are worthy, and listen to how I can use you to truly make a difference in the world." And with that Saul was blinded for three days.

Sometimes we have to be blinded, or blind-sided, by life and its circumstances before we'll listen to what God has to say to us. He created us to be used for His purposes, not to compare ourselves to someone else. We are to allow our Maker to work in our lives through our unique strengths and weaknesses.

I discovered that one characteristic God has had to fine tune in my life is my competitive spirit. As a young student, my energies were directed at my academics. I tried to always be at the top of my class. I didn't like it when someone else did better than me. I suppose it was a good thing that I geared my determined spirit toward school.

In my young adult life, I began to pick up a few sports. I learned to water ski in college. Though we didn't get to go too often, I was constantly wanting to improve, and eventually graduated to a single ski.

After we were married my husband and I were part of a co-ed volleyball league. I had played volleyball at camps and in P.E., but never at a competitive level such as this. I worked hard at getting better, and would become frustrated with myself when I blew it. It was even worse if my husband tried to "coach" me.

I joined a women's softball league in my early twenties. Again, outside of a picnic baseball game at the park, I had never played competitively. I worked my way from right field to left field, and was quickly coached on how to bunt properly. It seemed my full-swing hit would always go right to the short stop, but I was quick enough to get to first base on a nicely laid bunt.

Then, we had three sons, all of whom enjoyed athletics. They got their natural skills from their dad, who was a great athlete. They excelled in soccer, basketball, track, and football, and we were always there to root them on.

Now here's the hard part. I must confess to you that I would sometimes go to their games and become a completely different person. My fangs would grow, and I would become a monster bloodthirsty for triumph. It was so easy for me to get caught up in the moment of wanting to win, that, yes, I could become one of those "soccer moms" who was quite obnoxious on the sidelines. It's a good thing that I didn't drink or cuss, because I really felt like the referees needed my help at times, if you know what I mean.

I would come home and be totally exhausted from my efforts toward the boys' victories (or defeats, which were sometimes the case). I really didn't like my aggressive attitudes, and I would vow to do better next time. I saw my cutthroat behavior as a definite weakness, and an area where Satan had me bound.

The ultimate experience was at our oldest son's Junior Varsity basketball game against a cross-town rival. We were in the enemy's gym. Toward the end of the JV game the stands had become jammed with fans from both schools, anticipating the varsity game. Because there were so many people, some of the opposing team's crowd was sitting in very close proximity to where we were sitting. How dare they intrude?

In readiness for the big game, the other school had prepared what I affectionately call "weenie balloons." They were long and thin, and made a definite statement about which side you were backing. Each fan was given these balloons, bearing the school colors, to wave about in the air in support of their team. The lady in the seat below me held two of these lovely artifacts. Her son was also a Junior Varsity player.

The JV game had come down to the last seconds. The score was tied, and we had a chance to go ahead with a player at the free-throw line. In a deliberate, strategic move by the other team's coach, he had one of his players switch places with one of our players **after** the referee had given the ball to the free-throw shooter. Since players from both sides had illegally moved, it was whistled as a double foul, which negated any free-throw attempts. The possession arrow was in favor of the opposing team. They received the ball and drove down for the winning score.

We were in confused shock. What had just happened? Yet the ruling stood. The opposing side was cheering and waving their red and white balloons while we stood there in stunned silence. Suddenly, I noticed that in her excitement, the woman in front of me was unintentionally, but definitely, hitting me over and over again on the head with her wildly waving weenie balloon. My heart is pounding even now as I type this, and my shame still hits me in waves as I recall the incident. Before I knew what I was doing, I reached out, grabbed the object of offense, and popped it.

I was so embarrassed! Before she could even turn around to find out who the culprit was I jumped down on the stands beside her, put my arm around her shoulders and apologized with tears in my eyes. I'm sure she thought I was a lunatic, but I really didn't know what else to do. I congratulated her in my humiliated state for her son's win, and sat back down. I suppose I helped avoid a big fight, but what kind of "shining star" was I being to "a crooked and depraved generation"?

I wasn't sure if I should ever go to a sporting event again in my life. But here's what God showed me as I humbled myself before him and went back to an old friend, Philippians. "I can do everything through him who gives me strength" (Philippians 4:13). The converse of this is true also, "I can do nothing without him who gives me strength."

God also led me to write this personalized paraphrase from Philippians 3:4-14. It has become my testimony in some respects. I've always chuckled at the tongue-in-cheek pride Paul displayed as he wrote this passage. Hopefully, the same will be evident in my interpretation.

> *"If anyone thinks he has confidence in the flesh, I have more. I was born and raised in a pastor's home. We went to church twice*

on Sundays, once on Wednesdays, and I'm sure I never missed a revival meeting. I attended Point Loma Nazarene College and traveled throughout my summers singing at camps and churches. In regard to the law, I never attended a dance; as for zeal, I have faithfully served as choir member, Sunday school teacher, Vacation Bible School director and ladies' retreat chairman; as for legalistic righteousness, nearly faultless. (HA!)

"But none of this matters. My strivings are nothing. I consider everything a loss compared to the surpassing greatness of knowing Christ Jesus my Lord, for whose sake I have lost all things. My righteousness does not come from the things I have or haven't done. Those things are like trash--unless they are done as an outpouring of gratitude of what I have gained through Christ and his righteousness, which is found by faith in Him. I want to know Christ and the power of his resurrection. I want to participate in the fellowship of sharing in his sufferings—feeling the pain and hurt he experiences because of our sin and disobedience. I want to become like him in his death—dying to self and selfish gain, and loving others so much. And, so, somehow to attain the resurrection from the dead--abundant life on earth and eternal life in heaven.

"Not that I have already obtained all this, or have already been made perfect, but I press on to the goal which Christ originally set out for me in the first place—to be totally submitted to his will as an obedient servant of Him. Friends, I do not consider myself to have taken hold of it. But one thing I do: Forgetting what is behind (failures and successes, done with and settled), and straining on toward what is ahead, I press on toward the goal to win the prize for which God has called me heavenward in Christ Jesus."

I realized that I could ask for forgiveness, trust God for the weak areas of my life, and turn my competitive spirit over to him. He had to blind side me with a weenie balloon so I would listen to his will for my life. He said to me, "Jan, you are being passionate about the wrong things. I know you, I created you and every aspect of your personality. Now, shut your eyes to the things you think are worthy—success in sports, prevailing in your job, trying to be the best at everything for your own glory—and listen to what will really make a difference in the world. I want you to compete for the souls of the teens you are working with in the youth group right now. Pray without ceasing in the battle for their hearts and minds. I made you with a competitive spirit, so that I could use your strong-willed energy toward an uncompromising determination to do My will."

God changed Saul (who was also called Paul) from a persecutor of Christians to a powerful provider of the truth that Jesus is the Christ. He received a second name, a second chance, a grace and peace which is beyond all comprehension. Jesus does that for us, too. He didn't make me stop going to my boys' games. I've had second, third, and fourth chances, and I'm beginning to get it.

Did you catch the twist in Philippians 3:14? God is competitive, too. He is holding a prize for us, and He is encouraging us on toward our goal. We are on the winning team. We just need to keep pressing on. In the process of it all, He's working on our new name, "Victorious One."

Soil-Sifting Summary

- Our esteem does not come from within ourselves, but through Christ. What we need is not **self**-esteem, but **Christ**-esteem.
- You and I will never be God's equal, yet we try to play god in our own lives.
- Can you visualize it? People from every tribe and nation, speaking every language ever spoken on this earth, will be exalting Jesus as Lord. His very presence will cause us all to drop to our knees in honor of the One and Only King of Kings and Lord of Lords.
- We are called to share the joy that can be experienced by all who lay their sin at His feet and confess right now that Jesus is Lord.
- Sometimes we have to be blinded, or blind-sided, by life and its circumstances before we'll listen to what God has to say to us.
- I can do everything through Christ who strengthens me...I can do nothing without Him!
- God is competitive, too. He is holding a prize for us, and He is encouraging us on toward our goal. We are on the winning team.
- God is working on our new name, "Victorious One."

Digging into God's Word

- Philippians 1:6
- Philippians 2:5-8
- Philippians 2:9-11
- Philippians 2:14-16
- Acts 9:1-9
- Philippians 4:13
- Philippians 3:14
- 1 Corinthians 15:51-57

Extracting Truths and Treasures

Chapter 14

CROSSFIT

For God did not give us a spirit of timidity, but a spirit of power,
of love, and of self-discipline. 2 Timothy 1:7

My friend, Jenye, is a CrossFit enthusiast and participant. The title alone, "CrossFit," feels a little intimidating. A closer look, however, reveals that it is not about being a Ninja-Warrior type athlete performing crazy fetes. It is about coupling functional movement with good nutrition. It is an avenue by which you can lead a healthy, independent life and protect yourself against chronic disease and future incapacity. It is catered to each person's age, limitations, and strengths, while simultaneously challenging you toward tougher and more strenuous goals.

I remember when Jenye entered her first CrossFit competition, she requested prayer during our Bible study. She was filled with fear. She was almost paralyzed by the thought of facing her WODs (Workout of the Day). God had brought her so far in her emotional fears that stemmed from childhood abuse. Now she was learning that she also needed to surrender her physical fears, her physical being, to Him. She realized that though she loved physical activity, she was afraid of it, afraid of being pushed to the point of being hurt. This competition and the discipline it took to face it and go through with it, was the beginning of a bigger lesson and purpose God was preparing Jenye to accomplish for Him.

We went back a few years to understand her journey a little better. Jenye said she had always been fear-based. At one point she was even experiencing degrees of paranoia, where she didn't want to pick up the mail for fear of what it might contain. After her first husband died, she began to face her fear. Through counseling she began to identify this emotion that was controlling her. She learned to take her thoughts captive. She had worked long and hard to keep herself from living in the spirit of fear.

When she entered CrossFit that fear came rushing back. She wasn't really returning to the same struggles, but for some reason every time she went to her workouts, her stomach would be tied up in knots. It was the same feeling she had conquered emotionally, but now it was taking on its own life regarding her physical body. Rather than an emotional fear around an unknown situation, it was a fear over something that she had to do physically. One day while driving to CrossFit, she began to address the fear.

She began to think about what she was thinking about, advice she gives to counselees. She knew thoughts lead to feelings, so she began to explore those thoughts. She realized that every day on the way to the workouts, her self-talk would begin, "I can't do it. It's too hard What if I throw up? What if I can't finish?" No wonder she was so anxiety driven. Her errant thoughts were consuming her, but she was still finding herself fear-based.

Things actually started to get worse. There was a complete uneasiness that she couldn't pinpoint, except she kept feeling like it had something to do with God. That's when some flawed core beliefs she had about God started to rise up. One of her inaccurate convictions was that God would take away the things she loved.

Because of that belief, she had completely kept God out of CrossFit for the past two years.

Shortly after confronting this belief, Jenye got hurt from a repetitive exercise. Her coach told her she would need to cut way back on her workouts for a week or so. When Jenye got in her car she threw it back at God, "See! You win! Fine—take it away!" God spoke very clearly to her in response, "I don't want to take it. I want to be a part of it." She felt so loved at that moment, and began to ask God to show her what taking Him with her would look like.

During this season, Pastor Darren, lead pastor at Olive Knolls Church, was doing a series that included supporting our community (called #FORBAKO). Prior to this, as soon as she walked into the CrossFit door, God had not been welcome. Now she began to pray before CrossFit and in the middle of her WOD's. She started to talk more about God to other athletes. In spite of her conscious effort to include God in this part of her life, the foreboding feelings still did not go away. It was agonizing. She continued to seek God for what He wanted.

God finally revealed to her one Sunday in church that He wanted her to start a Bible study at CrossFit. She set out a fleece. If the owner said "yes" to the idea, Jenye would obey. If the owner said "no," she would not fight it. On Monday morning Jenye approached the owner with the idea of starting a Bible study. The owner looked at Jenye and said, "I have chills. Absolutely!"

That began the battle of "Am I good enough? Will people show up?" She made a flyer. All CrossFit gyms are called the Box because they are made up of four walls with no mirrors or sectioned-off rooms. It's a standard way of setting up CrossFit buildings, so Jenye called the Bible study, "Putting God in the Box." She decided to start with a study of *The Red Sea Rules* by Robert J. Morgan. The hardest part was that she knew everyone was in a different space. The CrossFit community is a wonderful, tight-knit, focused group of people. They are like-minded when it comes to training their bodies, but they don't necessarily include God in their activities. They seemed to want to learn more about faith, but they all came from such different backgrounds and belief systems. Jenye had to trust that God would go before her. As soon as Jenye said "Yes," the grip of fear that had been hanging on completely left.

The Bible study started out with about three people. It grew to up to seventeen. Saturday morning Bible study was a hard time for people to commit to since they were already arriving at CrossFit at 8:00. Jenye learned to be okay with whatever the numbers were. In the next study of the Parables, the people who showed up really needed more of the intimacy of a small discussion group. The stories Jesus told really exposed what you believed about Christ, and they were able to have deeper conversations with those who attended.

After the Parables were finished, the CrossFit boxes across the world began what is known as the Open. It is a major competition that gets people into the games. Jenye decided to take a break from Bible study during the Open because it was just too stressful. Through the five weeks of taking time off, Jenye prayed about the next study. She felt like she was receiving no direction. She thought maybe God was releasing her, saying that season was over for her. She really didn't think so because a really powerful foundation had been established. She just could not wrap her mind around what to do next.

Along the way, some of the women had approached Jenye about meeting with her to learn more. As the time was getting close to starting up again, one of the women coaches sent Jenye a text and asked if she would consider doing just a women's Bible study. Jenye and her husband had been leading together, and Jenye loved that, but she sensed that this was what was supposed to be. Immediately there was that sense of peace that God gives when we are falling in line with His will. She found a great Bible study: *Finding I am*, by Lysa TerKeurst.

As the first meeting approached, they decided to meet at one of the coach's houses. To Jenye's amazement, about ten women showed up. They began opening up and sharing about past church hurts. This vulnerability allowed some cracks to develop in some of the walls that had built up surrounding their faith in God. Jenye's prayer was, and continues to be, that they would discover who God is and that they would begin to understand His character.

Jenye works until 8:30 PM on Monday through Wednesday. The Bible study is on Thursday, and normally she would be so tired with one more night out. Instead, as Thursday night approaches, she becomes SOOO excited. She knows they are doing the right thing at the right time for this season. The owner is attending the study. She is asking for prayer to know how to run a Box that is godly in the predominantly worldly environment.

Jenye is receiving power from the Holy Spirit to do God's work. Her fears kept her on shaky ground for so long. As she continues to seek God and claim victory over her anxieties, God is helping her to remain on **solid ground**. God wants to be a part of our lives, whether in a "Box," behind a cubicle, or on a world-wide stage. He loves us, and He wants to fulfill His purpose through us wherever we may be.

Soil-Sifting Summary

- We must take our thoughts captive and make them obedient to Christ so that they don't maintain a stronghold against us.
- God doesn't necessarily want to take away what we love. He wants to be a part of it!
- When we seek God's will, He will reveal His way.
- We can trust that God will go before us and be with us.
- God's Word and His character begin to break down walls of hostility and confusion.
- Our fears, committed to Jesus, become strength and love and self-discipline through the Holy Spirit.

Digging into God's Word

- 2 Corinthians 10:3-5
- John 15:5
- Matthew 6:33-34
- Proverbs 16:9
- Ephesians 2:14-18
- 2 Timothy 1:7

Extracting Truths and Treasures

Chapter 15

LOCATION, LOCATION, LOCATION

The Lord had said to Abram, "Leave your country, your people
and your father's household and go to the land I will show you."
Genesis 12:1

$\mathcal{R}$eal estate agents often use the mantra, "Location,
location, location." The repetition of the word emphasizes
how important a home's locality really is. Desired sites for home
buyers seem to center around good school districts, scenic views,
proximity to recreation and nature, or walking distance to shopping
and entertainment. On the opposite end of the spectrum there are
factors that influence undesirable locations. Home value can
decrease if commercial or industrial buildings are too close; if the
home is near a freeway, railroad tracks, or flight path; or if the area
has a high crime rate.

In God's economy, the value of the location does not depend on
the world's interpretation. The places God wants us to go are often
a test of our obedience and faith. Abram is a perfect Old Testament
example of this type of confidence in God's trustworthiness. He was
called to leave his place of comfort and "go to a place he would later
receive as his inheritance...even though he did not know where he
was going. (Hebrews 11:8)" He obeyed and went! As a result we are
recipients of God's blessings.

My husband and his two brothers grew up around the central California coast. They always said that there were two places they would never live: Los Angeles and Bakersfield. The Lord has a great sense of humor, especially when we declare such statements of certainty. All three of them ended up in Bakersfield! God called them and they were obedient. It really wasn't as bad as the rap it usually gets from Hollywood. God located them where they could find work, raise their families, and be a blessing to others.

Several years ago, Debbie Hansen, the Children's Pastor at Olive Knolls Nazarene Church in Bakersfield, felt the call to "go." She was attending a ministerial class when she felt an urgency from the Spirit of God telling her to not wait for people to come to our church, but to go out to where they were located. She approached the pastor, presented her thoughts to the church board, and worked with the outreach pastor to determine where God was leading her.

After prayer and a little research, Debbie decided to start at a low-income apartment complex not too far from the church. Two weeks prior to the day she was planning to inquire about how our church could partner with the residents of the Springwood Apartments, a new manager had been hired. His charge by the company hiring him was to help build a sense of community with those living there, hopefully to reduce the tenant turn-over rate. He was a Christian man, who was answering a separate call, but God knew that he and Debbie would be talking! Of course, the partnership was welcomed. This began a connection that allowed the church to bring in Bible studies, dance classes, back-to-school events, skills training, and relationship building. These programs have continued for approximately the past ten years. The location was right. The step of faith was taken!

Debbie eventually transitioned from being Children's Pastor to becoming the Mission Pastor at Olive Knolls. God continued to develop His plan in Pastor Debbie's heart. She claimed a promise from Isaiah 61:1-4 for those God was bringing to her attention. Of particular note in verse 4 of that passage, she felt that God was assuring that He would "rebuild," "restore," and "renew" lives that had been "devastated for generations." Teams of people were created to reach out to other apartments and areas affected by poverty. Each week they serve food, meet needs, develop friendships, and take God's love to the needy. As a result, lives are being changed! God's promises are being fulfilled.

One of the strong visions Debbie had was to have a food truck that could serve free food. She envisioned this service to be one in which community could be built among those who came to partake. She actually sketched out a vehicle that was parked and ready, offering a variety of food and beverage choices. In front of the vehicle were tables and chairs arranged in an inviting setting, one that would encourage conversation and the sharing of prayer needs.

Debbie took the idea to prayer. Within a couple of weeks, she ran into a gentleman in the church kitchen one Sunday morning. This man and his wife were transitioning from a previous business venture and were wanting to sell their bus that had been converted to a coffee truck. The gentleman was intrigued by Debbie's ideas and they began to talk about the church possibly buying the food truck. She brought a proposal to the board, asking for about $20,000 for the purchase. She felt a little frustrated when a couple more weeks had passed and no decision had been made.

God's timing was as perfect as His locations! God had laid it on both the food truck owner's and his wife's heart to give the truck to the ministry, minus a $3000 cost they had invested to have cabinets installed. The vehicle, appraised for a much greater price, was being donated for a small fraction of its value! The ball (or bus in this case) was rolling! God was not through with this project yet!

Before the final decision was made and the board was still discussing licensing, registration, and maintenance costs, another miracle happened. Debbie's daughter, Cassie, had come to town for a visit. Debbie decided to take her for lunch at Moo Creamery. It was a pleasant day, and they were seated outside. Sitting at another table on the patio area were a couple of church members, Paul and his son, Jeremy. They were enjoying lunch with another gentleman that Debbie did not know.

Paul and his wife had reached out to Debbie and her kids when Debbie was traveling a broken road of divorce and family difficulty. They shared meals together. Debbie's son was allowed to use their computer for his school work. Paul's wife, Mary, would listen to Cassie, then five years old, as she read her kindergarten homework. They truly shared the love and care of Jesus with this little family!

During lunch, Paul shared the testimony of the Lord's healing and work in Debbie's and her kids' lives. The conversation led to the dream and vision for the coffee bus. The man who was eating lunch with Paul and Jeremy was a cattle rancher who actually supplied the Moo Creamery with beef. Paul bought Debbie and Cassie's lunch that day, which was a precious blessing. The Lord also worked in the rancher's heart to give $10,000 toward the coffee bus. This would cover the purchase, registration and licensing, and have money left over for supplies and maintenance purposes to get the project off to an amazing start.

If there was any skepticism up to this point, I think God was making it clear to the board that His hand was in the procuring of this food truck! The next issue for Debbie was location! She really felt like it was important to have a place where the food truck would be visible and easily accessible to the community. She reached a couple of dead ends. Feeling a little frustrated that she was not being a good steward of what God had provided, she and her team went to prayer.

Once again, God showed up, but not in the way they expected. He impressed on them as a collective group that he wanted them to put the truck on hold. He was leading them to conduct Bible studies at an apartment property that was in deteriorating condition. There was little hope that there would be any maintenance on these properties by the owners. There was even less hope for the physical, emotional, and spiritual conditions of the residents, outside of Jesus.

With fear and trembling, in absolute humble obedience, they set up their first Tuesday Bible study. Feeling like it would be a success if one or two showed up, they were surprised to have seventeen in attendance under a little pop-up tent with folding chairs. They have continued to be available for prayer and Bible teaching, extending the hope of Jesus to the poor, the brokenhearted, the captives of sin and defeat (See Isaiah 61:1). Recently a family from this ministry was baptized at our church. They are a "planting of the Lord for the display of his splendor. (Isaiah 61:3)" It will be exciting to come alongside them and watch as they continue to grow in the Lord and turn around the generational devastation they have experienced.

As Debbie continues to seek God's will and timing, I am confident that He will provide the perfect location for them. He knows location—His location—is everything! In the meantime, He continues to work through the obedience and faith of His followers to create new life! Debbie shared that one of these miraculous creations, named Tina, completely "wrecked" her.

When Debbie met Tina she had been living in the Springwood Apartments for about two weeks. This was the first ever home outside of institutions and rehabilitations that Tina had ever known. Tina grew up in an abusive home. At age ten she was admitted to a mental institution by her parents, who were afraid of being exposed for their abuse. Tina continued to be abused by some of the workers at the hospital. When she retaliated by biting one of them, her teeth were pulled out, with no anesthesia. Tina was twelve. She was emancipated from the mental hospital at age nineteen. On the streets, she turned to drugs. She was in and out of prison, until a judge ordered rehabilitation.

Tina's mom strangely got involved and found a Christ-centered rehabilitation center in Kern County called Tabitha's House, run by a woman named Ms. Bennie. The social worker that dropped Tina off told Ms. Bennie that Tina was an animal and would never be rehabilitated. Why did Tina's mom choose this location? Because location is everything! God knew that Ms. Bennie would not give up on Tina. It was rough. Tina was violent and angry. She was uneducated and bent on lashing out at anyone and everyone in her way.

Over the next fourteen years, Ms. Bennie and her husband loved Tina. They cared for her, taught her to read and write, and sang and spoke Scripture over her. Eventually the walls began to crumble. Tina could not deny that God had sent her to this place, to these people, to be shown a love that she had never known before. She invited Jesus into her life, and she became a new creation.

Now God placed Debbie in her life. She attended Bible studies, helped in the children's ministry at church, and found continued comfort and love through new friends. This former illiterate adult was given the gift of poetry. When Tina passed away recently, Debbie gathered some of her poems and put them in a little booklet.

As I read them, I was the one who was "wrecked." If God could take Tina's life and plant it on the **solid ground** of His redeeming work on the cross, my faith could no longer be stagnant. God is the God of miracles. May these stories, and this poem of Tina's, give your faith a new anchor!

I AM GRATEFUL

By Tina Clark

I am grateful everyday
To know you are my God
And I am your child.
Lord I give you
Praise and honor.
Every day you shine your
Light and love in my life,
You have blessed me beyond my mental belief.
Even when I am at my
Lowest you show out your best.
I love you Jesus
And I know you love me too.
I am honored to be called
A child of God and a joint
Heir with Christ.
Thank you Father God for never giving up on me
Through and through.
How can I be a better servant to you Lord?
Use me, Father God, I am a willing
Vessel to help others, to serve others according
To your will.
In Jesus name I pray amen.

Soil-Sifting Summary

- When God tells us to "go," we need to be obedient, even when we're not sure of the location.
- God promises that He will "rebuild," "restore," and "renew" lives that had been "devastated for generations."
- We should be available for prayer and Bible teaching, extending the hope of Jesus to the poor, the brokenhearted, the captives of sin and defeat.
- When you invite Jesus into your life you become a new creation.

Digging into God's Word

- Genesis 12:1
- Hebrews 11:8
- Isaiah 61:1-4
- 2 Corinthians 5:17

Extracting Truths and Treasures

Chapter 16
STEP BY STEP

[He] redeems your life from the pit and crowns you with love
and compassion. Psalm 103:4

𝔗his is a story about human trafficking. It is a hard story, but one filled with God's healing and redemption. In order to understand the depths of God's amazing love, we need to get a glimpse of the depravity of sin in our world. I cried when I heard this story. I cried when I listened to it and again when I wrote it. At the same time, I rejoiced in a life that was brought out of the pit of despair.

The term "human trafficking" is considered a modern term. It is equivalent to modern day slavery. It is estimated that there are more than 21 million human trafficking victims world-wide. Human trafficking is the exploitation of a person through force, fraud, or coercion. It can be abuse through sex, forced labor, or domestic servitude. Human trafficking is the second largest growing segment of organized crime in the United States. It is a growing problem in our nation, our counties, and our cities.

Bakersfield is a hub for human trafficking. Bakersfield's location connects a route both north and south through California via Highways 5 and 99, and it is also a convenient meeting point for the road to Las Vegas. Bakersfield's Human Services reported 139 child exploitation cases in 2018. These are only the reported cases because people are often ashamed or afraid to report their perpetrator. It is often known as the hidden or silent crime, but it is time we shine some light on it.

As Christians it starts with awareness. Knowing there are people who are in our circles who may be victims and being sensitive to their lack of self-worth is a beginning. Connecting our ministries with faith-based organizations that are working toward helping restore these victims is also crucial. Partnering with nonprofits who are extending counseling and support for men, women, and children who have grown up knowing nothing different is still another means of action. Yet another way might be to join local coalitions to increase awareness and effect policy change in our legal system.

Diana is one of those people who is a champion for this cause. Her non-profit organization, Hope Rising (more information about this is at the end of the chapter), reaches out to young girls who are in foster care or juvenile hall. Some are referred by a concerned friend or family member who have seen signs of possible sexual abuse. Diana is passionate about this issue because she has lived it. She is gloriously on the other side of her pain and brokenness, and God is giving her avenues to turn her past anguish into a lifeline of hope. She was graciously willing to share her story.

Diana's earliest recollection of her father was being sexually abused by him at a very young age. He was actually a preacher in a Christian church that has some cult-like qualities, but he definitely lived a separate life in public than in private. His abuse continued through her school-aged years. When she was about seven, he began taking her on "errands," in which he would offer her to other men for sexual pleasure for money. There was an elder in the church who had arranged her marriage with his son, who was getting his sexual training on her. This was to occur when she turned eighteen.

Her mom ran a daycare. If she knew of what was going on, she turned a blind eye. It was ungodly to question or go against your husband. Because Diana was the oldest, she was given a myriad of chores and responsibilities, beyond her years. She would care for her younger siblings and do household chores. She would also help her mom with the children in the daycare. All of this was Diana's "normal." Her community consisted of her family and her church. She knew nothing different.

Diana went to a small private school which tended to shelter her from the truth. It wasn't until she was out of junior high, in a large public high school, that she began to really question the things that had been happening to her. A friend made her go talk to the counselors. Diana said that they were wonderful to her. Diana desperately wanted to talk about her situation. She wanted the words to spill out. However, because of the extreme trauma and lack of sex education, her brain didn't have the words or the tools to talk about the sexual abuse. She was convinced that if her dad found out she had talked about him that he would kill her. He had also used fear tactics and torture to convince her that she wasn't good enough or had not done enough for him.

Eventually, Diana had a complete breakdown. She couldn't function! She opened up to some extended family about some of her father's abuse. They had a family meeting and confronted her dad. He said he had to punish Diana like that because she was such an unruly child, but that he loved her and thought this was what was best for her. Her grandparents suggested that Diana live with her aunt and uncle for a year, in a city away from her parents. Though they were non-abusive, they were also a part of the same denomination. It was a much better environment all around, but Diana began to question God and religion. She was angry and disillusioned.

During this time she attended a Christian high school. She actually got to experience some semi-normal teenage experiences like going to lunch with friends and going on a skiing trip, things she had never been able to do before. The Vice Principal and his wife asked her over for dinner, invited her for coffee, and generally took a special interest in her. She couldn't understand it. Shouldn't they be pouring out their attention on all of their star students instead of this crazy girl? Through their unconditional love the first rays of light began to penetrate the chink in the armor that she had built around herself. She remembers being "freaked out" as she watched the loving dynamics between the husband and wife and their little girl. Since she had never experienced anything like this, it was like being in a foreign country and culture.

For her senior year, it was deemed that she should move back home. She now knew she could never go back. When she resisted her father's advances and demands, she was kicked out on the street. She was seventeen, homeless, alone, with nowhere to go. She knew she needed a job. She ended up getting hired at Olive Knolls Christian School as a preschool aide. The teacher she worked with was a God-send. Joyce had grown up in the same denomination. They would find themselves comparing notes, bonding over similar backgrounds, and giggling hilariously over some of the ridiculous things they had encountered. Diana was nowhere close to being healed, but God was preparing the ground and guiding her steps along the way.

Despite her anger at God, she sensed the "hound of heaven" pursuing her. This phrase came from a 17th century poem by Francis Thompson describing the pursuit of the Holy Spirit that was relentless on his life. The word picture here is one of God not giving up on us, like the Shepherd looking for His lost sheep. She felt strongly that she should attend church. She began to go to Valley Bible Church, where she accepted Christ and was baptized.

Over time Diana was invited to live in a healthy home for a few years. She attended Bible studies and classes, but still felt frustrated and broken. She couldn't understand why Christianity seemed to work for everyone else, but it wasn't working for her. She started college, pursuing a degree in early childhood education. She always had a heart for kids, but she had no tools for working with them. She certainly had not received proper modeling or nurturing during her formative years. She learned so much from the teachers she worked with daily. They taught her how to harness her love for kids in a positive way. She learned how to comfort them when they got an "owie," how to wipe away their tears, and how to teach them their letters. It was a real healing time for her.

These were all steps toward where God was leading her. It was during a Franklin Graham Crusade in Bakersfield that God really revealed His plan. After the crusade there was a huge youth rally. Diana remembers enjoying the time with friends and people she had met and known through the years. When the crowds began to disperse, she found herself sitting and praying in a building. There was a door on the other side of the room that was cracked open. She could see light peeking through. God revealed to her that the door was symbolic of her life. It was just beginning to be cracked open. She could see what looked like steps leading toward the door. He let her know that there were some hard things she was going to have to do to get there, but He had something for her on the other side. In the service before that they had said to make a circle around yourself and start by asking God to change you. Diana did that and said, "Change me!"

Those steps were slow and steady. She tried a couple of Christian counselors, but they didn't know how to help her. They hadn't had training for cases like hers. Finally she was connected to an organization called Passionate Hearts. Through this group she received some excellent mentoring that started her journey toward facing her issues head on. She was able to begin talking about the abuse of her dad, and allowing her Heavenly Father to fill those places of bitterness, sorrow, and pain.

She was now attending Olive Knolls Church. One Sunday morning, she was feeling so frustrated and so broken, she actually wrote her need on a prayer request card. The next day she got a call from one of the pastors who recommended a counselor named Jennifer Anderson. She wasn't sure how another counselor might help her, but she decided to make an appointment. It was obvious that God had led her steps to this very woman for such a time as this. Jennifer had been through a childhood of sexual abuse as well. She helped Diana begin to do the incredibly difficult work of rebuilding her life. She literally had to go back and parent herself from infancy on up. She had to face each trauma, but first she had to talk about the traumas. Slowly, over a season of heart-wrenching reflection, allowing God to demolish the strongholds of her past, and rebuilding the person God had intended for her to be, she found freedom. She began to grasp and believe God loved her. She began to love herself.

Today Diana is healthy and whole. She had two major goals as she was walking through her journey. The first one was that she could have a healthy family of her own. She is happily married with two great children. The second desire was that she would be able to help others whose lives were shattered to become complete. She pursued and earned a degree in crisis counseling, giving her expert tools, coupled with her personal understandings, to best be able to help those who have experienced trauma. God has allowed Diana to speak up and down the state bringing hope to victims and awareness to communities through a great organization called Runaway Girl. When she became weary of traveling away from her family during the week, she decided to start her own non-profit. That way she could work locally in a mission field that is in great need of workers.

What an amazing story of redemption. God raised her out of the pit onto **solid ground**, and has crowned her with love and compassion!

If you or someone you know is a victim of human trafficking, please call this National Hotline.
1 (888) 373-7888

Diana's organization:
Diana Cisneros, Director of Hope Rising
Consultant CSEC Action Team
Human Trafficking Trainer and Advocate

Soil-Sifting Summary

- Our unconditional love toward others might just be the first light to penetrate a chink in the armor that they have built around themselves.
- Like the "Hound of Heaven" or the Good Shepherd, God does not give up on us. He continues to pursue us until we are found.
- God often leads us step-by-step to His open door. He has a plan for us on the other side, and He will be with us through the process.
- God desires for us to live a life of complete freedom through Jesus.
- God redeems us from the pit onto **solid ground**, and crowns us with love and compassion.

Digging into God's Word

- 1 Corinthians 13
- Ezekiel 34:11-16
- Psalm 37:23-24
- 2 Corinthians 3:17-18
- Psalm 103:1-5

Extracting Truths and Treasures

Chapter 17

HORN OF SALVATION

The Lord is my rock, my fortress, and my deliverer; my God is my rock, in whom I take refuge. He is my shield and the horn of my salvation, my stronghold. Psalm 18:2-3

𝓛ong before Keith was released from prison, he was delivered! Keith is a member of our church (Olive Knolls Church), a participant in Celebrate Recovery (CR) on Friday nights, a business owner, and a poet. When anyone hires Keith to paint their house or business, one of the first things Keith does is shares his written testimony. His desire is to be open about his past so that there will be no room for future accusations or repercussions.

Keith had a broken childhood of sexual and emotional abuse. He was placed into foster care, developed a deep-seated dislike for all men, and lashed out at classmates. He shunned social contact to avoid more of the rejection he had lived with up to this point in his life. He experimented with drugs over the years, but was mostly content to just be a "pothead." The escape that marijuana provided from his reality was welcomed, though temporary.

Keith worked hard to make a buck. He eventually got married, and "played church" to appease his wife and her family. All the while, by minimizing what had happened to him and ignoring God's wooing on his life to be freed from sin, pain, and his unforgiving spirit, he found himself entering into a generational cycle. He touched his step daughter in an impure way. Immediately he knew that he had abused the authority he had been entrusted with in her life. Racked with guilt, he wished he had never been born. He briefly considered suicide, but instead decided to take responsibility for what he had done. Ultimately, he turned himself into the police, and found himself in prison. He was sure he had signed his own death warrant.

The day he turned himself in, he got down on his knees, on the cold concrete floor of his cell, and for the first time, gave his heart and life to Jesus. No more "playing church" or just giving Christ lip-service. This time he meant it! He surrendered everything to God, realizing that his way of running his own life was NOT working. He began to study the Bible and to seek God's plan for his life. Through God's power and grace he made it through his sentence, clean and sober, and ready for whatever was ahead. The "old" Keith had never had an interest in poetry, but God started filling Keith's head with amazing words that he loves to share with others. They give you a glimpse of his heart and his soul. This one was written, revised, and finished while in federal prison.

JUST FAITH

His salvation rescued me.
My sins are gone. My soul is free.
But I've hurt people, my Lord.
There's things that I must make up for.
For the pain that I've beset,
Please show me how to pay my debt.
From high up in His judgment seat,
He pointed earthward, toward my feet.
Into a great pit I did stare,
His booming voice said, "JUMP IN THERE."
Deep in the pit, no light or sound.
The very thought made my heart pound.

If that's the way, Lord, I will try.
But promise me that I won't die.
"NO PROMISE WILL I MAKE TO THEE.
HAVE FAITH WHAT HAPPENS' MEANT TO BE."
The pain I've caused I so despise.
I spread my arms and closed my eyes.
I put my faith in God above.
I bent my knees and gave a shove.
I dared not think where I might land.
Then on my arm, I felt His hand.
I opened my eyes and there I stood
On **solid ground** and all was good.
He said, "MY SON, I'VE CLEARED YOUR SIN.
WATCH WHERE YOU'RE GOING,
NOT WHERE YOU'VE BEEN."

KAPoe

Keith learned over time to depend on God as his rock, his fortress, and his deliverer. He grew to know God as his refuge, his shield, his stronghold, and the horn of his salvation. When the Bible refers to the horn, or horn of salvation, there are several connotations. The first comes from the story of Abraham and Isaac in Genesis 22. God provided a ram, caught by its horns in the thicket, to be the sacrifice in place of Isaac. As the horn of our salvation, Jesus secured Himself as our sacrifice and gave His life as a ransom for us. Keith received Jesus and accepted His sacrificial gift!

Another purpose of the horn in Biblical context was a container for anointing oil (see 1 Samuel 16:13). As our horn of salvation, God has anointed us with His Holy Spirit through Christ. The Holy Spirit of God has anointed Keith's life through his poetry, through his work, and through his ministry.

Finally, the horn was used as an instrument to lead God's people into victory (see Joshua 6:13, 20). God is in the business of winning our battles. His presence in our lives and our obedience to Him leads us into victorious living! Though the journey hasn't been easy, Keith is continuing to learn to walk in victory!

While in prison, Keith's poetry became his ministry. The words flowed straight from God to the page. One day a woman named Sister Shirley visited Keith's prison in search of poems written by inmates. She was hoping to print a book containing a conglomerate of the men's poems. Another inmate pointed at Keith, and said, "He writes poetry, and he's pretty good, too!" Sister Shirley asked to see Keith's poems. A few days later, Keith was called out of his cell into the day room. Sister Shirley asked him a pointed question. She wanted to know if Keith had really written the poems or if he had taken them out of a book. She apologized for asking, but she wanted the truth. Keith saw it as a compliment that she obviously saw his poetry as good enough to be in a book.

Sister Shirley asked Keith if he would continue to write for the prison ministry. Keith began taking requests from the men to give him subject ideas. He would send Sister Shirley his completed writing, and she would publish it for the prison men. Keith said if it wasn't for Sister Shirley he would probably have half a dozen poems in a shoe box under his bed. She gave him an outlet and the encouragement to write. He has over 400 poems to this day, published and illustrated in two books.

Keith got out of prison in 2008. He continued to write poetry, became involved in church and Bible studies, and worked on furthering his education. He loved gaining knowledge and learning more about the Lord. His parole period kept him in Kern County, so when his ankle bracelet came off, he was thrilled to take a day trip with his good friend, Don. Don, a retired school teacher, was able to fill the trip up to the Sierras with a lot of scientific and environmental knowledge.

Their fellowship was blessed by God as they took in the giant sequoias and enjoyed some beautiful scenic stops. They visited the Trail of 100 Giants where Keith had Don take his picture next to an immense sequoia. Though the tree dwarfed Keith's size, it oddly spoke to Keith of their similarities. The massive tree had withstood several lightning strikes, fires, wind and water erosion, and even some insect infestations. Its scars ran deep and black, but these marks only added to the uniqueness and beauty of the creation. Many of Keith's scars also ran deep and black. Because of the grace of God, he knew he had been transformed into a unique and beautiful creation as well. The tree inspired the following poem.

SCARS

There was a young and tender heart
That love had never known.
There was no one to share its life.
And so it was alone.
Abused and hated by its own.
An object of disgrace.
It struggled in an angry world
To find and have a place.
So it became a bitter heart

That love had never known.
And hatred thrived inside the heart
Until it turned to stone.
And though the heart knew right from wrong,
It knew not how to care.
So it lashed out at all around,
It's bitterness to share.
It scarred the evil and the good,
The innocent and true.
But every scar its anger caused
Left scars upon it too.
God's Spirit was relentless
Through the pain it shared and felt.
And finally, one golden day,
The heart began to melt.
And so the heart, with all its scars
Fell down at Jesus' feet.
And soon its scars began to heal,
And bitter tears turned sweet.
It prayed, "Dear Lord, how can I heal
The scars I've caused to them"?
He said, "Like you, they must come near
And they must touch My hem."
The heart was filled with Jesus' love.
That made the heart to grow.
And soon it shared with all around
The love that it now knows.
The heart now tender as it was
The day that it was born.
For Jesus healed its many scars
Of hatred, pain, and scorn.
He takes the dark and tortured hearts,

And makes them shining stars.
He holds them up for all to see.
But some just see the scars.

KAPoe

Another stop for Keith and Don was Dome Rock. It is similar to Half Dome in Yosemite National Park. Dome Rock in Sequoia National Forest is a large dome made of granite that allows for some stunning views of The Needles, a series of enormous granite spires, and the forest laid out below. Keith and Don did not attempt to do any rock climbing off-trail, but they did build some stone altars. Don had lost his wife to cancer, and Keith's ex-wife wanted nothing to do with him. On their drive up, they had shared deeply and vulnerably of their desire to be married again someday. They each placed a stack of varied-sized rocks together and prayed for each other. Their memorial altars indicated their gratefulness to God for helping them thus far, as well as a plea to bless their futures. By the end of that year, they both had started to date the woman they each eventually married. (For more on building altars, see Chapter 24, "Our Cornerstone.")

Keith's studies have resulted in a Bible college degree. He also currently has a chaplaincy certificate which helps yield permission to go into local prisons. He conducts Bible studies with the incarcerated men. They listen closely to what Keith has to say. Not only does he have the "credentials" to share, but he has the experience and the heart. He can talk to them about pride and forgiveness because he has lived it. He encourages them and tries to prepare them for the difficulty of parole. He continues his poetry, which is often rather frank and to the point. The prisoners accept the words more easily sometimes than those outside the prison walls. He doesn't apologize. He just asks people, "Did it offend you, or did it convict you?"

Keith has become a new creation in Christ, and most people love and accept him for who he is becoming. A few cannot get past the place of judgement. Keith fought sharing his testimony with Diana (see Chapter 16, "Step by Step"), but he felt compelled by God to have her read it. When he didn't hear back from her for a few weeks, he was sure she had found him repulsive. Instead, Diana was grateful to know that God was transforming someone on the other side of her story. Over time, this unlikely pair have become like brother and sister. Each of them has become a part of the other's healing. Only God could orchestrate a relationship such as this! May you be challenged through Keith's story and this final poem to look for the fruit in the lives of others!

NEW

I wished that I could change my past.
The Lord said, "Follow me."
I asked how I could earn such grace.
He said, "My gift is free."
But God, my life is stained by sin.
And all the world has seen.
He said, "I sent my son to earth.
His blood will wash you clean.
If Christians hate the things you've done,
That's good, so don't despair.
But if it's you they cannot love,
Bring them to me in prayer.
Your 'old man' is a fearsome thing.
But that's no longer you.

If they will judge you by your fruit
They'll see I've made you new."

KAPoe

Soil-Sifting Summary

- Jesus secured Himself as our sacrifice and gave His life as a ransom for us.
- God has anointed us with His Holy Spirit through Christ
- God is in the business of winning our battles. His presence in our lives and our obedience to Him leads us into victorious living!
- Jesus heals our wounds, and He transforms our scars into "shining stars."
- We need to remember the times that God has helped us thus far, and pray, believing that He will bless our future.
- We should not judge people because of their past, but look for the fruit in their lives.

Digging into God's Word

- Genesis 22:13; Mark 10:45
- 1 Samuel 16:13; 1 John 2:20
- Joshua 6:13, 20; 1 John 5:4
- Psalm 107:19-22; Proverbs 4:18
- I Samuel 7:7-14
- Matthew 7:1-5

Extracting Truths and Treasures

Chapter 18

KEEPING IN STEP

Since we live by the Spirit, let us keep in step with the Spirit.
Galatians 5:25

We walk for many reasons. We sometimes walk for exercise. We often use our strides to get from point "A" to point "B." We stroll through the park to enjoy the spring breeze or fall colors. We march with purpose to our child's room to give them a needed lecture. We carry our important documents from our office space to the boss's office for a signature or approval. Our physical steps are crucial to our daily routines and activities, but are we walking in step with the Spirit?

Mike Underwood's job included multiple daily paces. He recently retired from a position as a letter carrier with the United States Postal Service. Through rain, sleet, snow, and hail—and Bakersfield's triple-digit summer temperatures—Mike trekked through his assigned neighborhoods. He made sure each home had the important, and sometimes not-so-important, posted letters, circulars and bills. Whether junk mail or certified documents, Mike, along with his fellow couriers, was dedicated to making sure mail was delivered in a timely and efficient manner. His steps were important!

Besides his daily steps for work each day, Mike was keeping in step with the Spirit. Because Mike maintained a close relationship with Christ, God was bringing another purpose to his steps. About a year before Mike retired, he felt compelled by God to pray and fast for a friend's need. After a day of walking his routes to bring mail to the constituents, he began to circle a particular set of neighborhood blocks for a completely different reason. He was praying for a miracle as a step of faith. Doing a prayer walk was part of the commitment.

Two things were happening simultaneously. First, in one of the Bible studies Mike and his wife attended, they had been using *Discipled by Jesus* by Hal and Debbi Perkins as a guideline for going through God's Word. As they analyzed and personalized scripture and applied it to their lives, they were using five questions to filter their thoughts. These questions are ones that Jesus asked His own disciples while walking and talking with them during His ministry on earth: "1) Who do you say I am? 2) Do you understand what I have done for you? 3) Are you listening to me? 4) Do you truly love me? 5) Do you believe me?"[2] Mike felt that God was asking Him to put action to his faith. He was sensing that God wanted to know if He really believed God was who He said He was.

To take this thought a little further, Jesus revealed His character and sovereignty throughout the Old and New Testaments. God told Moses, "I Am who I Am" (Exodus 3:14). He was declaring Himself as our faithful and dependable God who is worthy of complete trust and worship. We can fully claim these comforting, powerful, and authoritative "I Am's:"
- I am the Good Shepherd (Psalm 23)
- I am the One who forgives, heals, and redeems (Psalm 103:3-4)
- I am Wonderful Counselor, Mighty God, Everlasting Father, Prince of Peace (Isaiah 9:6b)

---

[2] Perkins, Hal and Debbi. *Discipled by Jesus.* Denver, Colorado: Outskirts Press, 2013.

- I am the Bread of Life (John 6:35)
- I am the Way, the Truth and the Life (John 14:6)
- I am the King of Kings and Lord of Lords (Revelation 17:14)

We are called and challenged through life's circumstances to put our trust in these amazing attributes of God!

Mike was challenged to place his faith in the almighty healing God. How was this going to look? In a second Bible study, on a separate evening of the week, Mike's life group was studying Mark Batterson's *Draw the Circle.* In one of the video sessions, Batterson spoke about doing a 4.7-mile prayer walk around Capitol Hill. He was claiming the area and the people for God. He believed that God had called him to start a church in the residential neighborhood surrounding the capitol buildings in Washington D.C., and by praying around the perimeter of the area, Batterson was laying his faith on the line. God showed Himself faithful to Batterson's prayers. In the years after Batterson's prayer walk, their church has grown into one church with seven locations. All of the properties that they own are within the circle that he walked.

Mike's life group was encouraged to circle their problems and requests in prayer. It was both a metaphorical and physical way to express belief in God's power and promises. Mike asked himself, "Why not? We serve God, so why not ask and trust and believe?" It was a way that Mike could tangibly put his faith into action. He began to implement his plan. He wanted to bring glory to God and not draw attention to anything he was doing, so he initially didn't tell anyone about his idea, except his wife. When he got off work he would start his trek. He had decided to fast as a part of this journey. He chose to do the Daniel fast, consisting of mostly lentils, lettuce, tomatoes, water and juice. He chose twenty-one days as his time frame. He mapped out a route of several blocks around the neighborhood of the person he was praying for.

Mike's prayer focus was for Marilyn Illingworth, one of the participants in his Wednesday night Bible study. Marilyn had shared a prayer request over several months about some extreme pain in her right ankle and foot. The doctor treating her said it was arthritis. She was given a cortisone shot, and finally was put in a brace. The brace provided some relief for a time, but other problems surfaced as she compensated with other muscle groups. The discomfort and pain was so bad that it was affecting her quality of life. She was helping her kids by watching some of her young grandkids, and it was difficult to maintain the routine when she was hurting all of the time.

Each Wednesday night, her prayer request was the same: Relief from her foot and ankle pain. God had laid Marilyn on Mike's heart. His prayer as he circled the block was focused on that specific request. He always started his prayer walk with the Lord's Prayer. After that, he centered in on Marilyn's foot. As other thoughts popped in, he would push them aside to keep his attention on the precise request of healing Marilyn's foot. He laughed as he thought about how he had never before prayed so explicitly and intensely about a particular part of the body. The first week he walked the block once. The second week he went around twice, and the third week he walked it three times. He prayed for God's will and for His timing and purpose to be revealed.

At the end of the twenty-one days, Mike wasn't sure how to wrap things up. He didn't know if anything had happened. About a week before he had completed the prayer commitment, he had shared with Marilyn that he was praying for her foot. She felt humbled that God would care enough about her to raise up an intercessor. Before she started seeing any results, she claimed the healing. It wasn't immediate, but over the process of the next weeks and months, complete healing took place. Marilyn even shared with her doctor that someone had been praying for her foot, and she believed it had been healed. An irreversible diagnosis of arthritis had been reversed by God. There was no other explanation. The huge trial of enduring pain for most of the previous year had been lifted.

Mike's faith was strengthened tremendously, along with those in the small group who had shared the prayer request. Mike mentioned how he was amazed that God would answer the prayers of someone like himself. He felt "insignificant" in the grand scheme of things. Yet, in God's kingdom there is no caste system, no one is insignificant. In fact, the mighty men and women of the Bible were terribly flawed. Gideon was afraid. Moses stuttered. Rahab was a prostitute. Abraham was too old. Martha worried about everything.

None of these people did great things for God because of their own significance. They did amazing things because God had called them and they obeyed. Pastor Tom Neary, who has a blog called Pastor Unlikely, put it this way, "God doesn't call the qualified, he qualifies the called." He just wants us to trust Him completely. Mike answered God's call. He believed and claimed the verse, "Ask and it will be given to you; seek and you will find; knock and the door will be opened to you" (Matthew 7:7).

How amazing that God spoke into the heart of Mike for this specific miracle. Mike had to be in step with the Spirit in order to hear the Spirit speak to him. Are you listening to Him? When you allow yourself to get so busy with your own sense of direction, you might miss letting God do His work in and through you. Keep on walking—for health, to complete a task, to reach a destination. Just make sure that no matter what your reasons are for walking, you are keeping in step with the Spirit of God!

Soil-Sifting Summary

- Our physical steps are crucial to our daily routines and activities, but are we walking in step with the Spirit?
- Jesus revealed His character and sovereignty throughout the Old and New Testaments with "I AM" statements. Do we really believe God is who He says He is?
- In God's kingdom there is no caste system. No one is insignificant. He just wants us to trust Him completely. He hears our cries. We need to do our part in faith and trust— asking, seeking, and knocking.
- When you allow yourself to get so busy with your own sense of direction, you might miss letting God do His work in and through you.

Digging into God's Word

- Galatians 5:25
- Exodus 3:14
- Psalm 23, Psalm 103, John 6, John 14, Revelation 17
- Galatians 3:26-29
- Matthew 7:7-8
- Colossians 3:23-24

Extracting Truths and Treasures

_____

_____
_____
_____
_____
_____
_____
_____
_____
_____
_____
_____
_____
_____
_____
_____
_____
_____
_____
_____
_____
_____
_____
_____
_____
_____
_____
_____

Chapter 19
THE TRUE PRIZE

Do you not know that in a race all the runners run, but only one
gets the prize? Run in such a way as to get the prize.
1 Corinthians 9:24

In the early years of the 21st century, there was a group of eight to ten fun, energetic women who would get up at 4:30 AM to arrive at the Olive Knolls Church workout room for a 5:00 AM class. Together we did step aerobics, circuit training, and strength training exercises. Sarah (Hughes) Botts, Cindy Carver, and Jackie Holmes were a few of my crazy friends who joined me to try to keep physically active and healthy. I will always have a special place in my heart for these ladies who were disciplined, dedicated, and willing to try just about anything I threw at them. We sharpened and pushed each other to go one step farther, do one more push-up, or perform one more rep.

We had Sarah looking marvelous for her December wedding in 2007. Cindy and I successfully kept from putting on too many pre-menopausal pounds. Jackie, though she may not have known it, was preparing for future marathons. The best part of these mornings, however, was sharing our prayer requests and lifting our work, our families (and future families), and our needs before our Creator. Our physical discipline seemed to hone our spiritual discipline.

Over time, we stopped meeting for our morning exercise fix. The aerobic and weight rooms were needed for school classrooms after the Olive Knolls Christian School (OKCS) fire. Sarah was starting her "little" family (now up to eight kids). My job position was shifting to more of an administrative role. As often happens, life changed, and we entered a new season.

During this time, Jackie had participated in a few 5K runs. In 2013, challenged by her daughters, she ran her first half marathon. She has been entering races ever since, pulling her husband, Allen, into the fray. Jackie had noticed on Pastor Joe's (Halbert) Facebook page that he ran in a marathon every year for an organization called World Vision. Jackie was intrigued and decided it might be fun to join him and his team. Always having been mission-minded, she thought this would be a perfect way to mesh her love for missions with her love for running. The more she researched it, the more she felt led by the Lord to start a team from Bakersfield, specifically a group from Olive Knolls Church.

As happens more often than not, when God is in the plans he goes ahead of us and prepares the path. When Jackie spoke to Pastor Darren about the possibility of a World Vision team, Darren was immediately excited. He had been praying about finding someone who would champion and organize this very thing! Jackie got in touch with the director of World Vision and started the ball rolling. The purpose of the World Vision yearly marathon is to raise money and awareness of the need for water in Africa. Fifty dollars of sponsorship money provides life-changing clean water to children in need. Along with training for the race, the participants also try to raise money through donations of friends and family.

Jackie explained that training for a marathon is hard. There are times when your legs are hurting, your stomach is hurting, and your head is hurting. You have to get comfortable with the pain in order to grow and prepare. But for Jackie, the training for the race was easy compared to the discomfort of having to fundraise. She was always the kid whose family ended up eating and paying for all of the candy bars that were being sold for a school fundraiser because Jackie just did not like soliciting people to give money. Even when it is for a good cause, like water for children, it was stretching and humbling her to seek sponsors to support her efforts.

To help me understand how various aspects of life overlap in purpose and direction, Jackie explained a video she watched in a Diversity and Counseling class she taught at Fresno Pacific University. The video was of Melody Hobson, chairwoman of Dream Works and wife of George Lucas. In her video, she was explaining how a former swimming coach of hers had kept pushing her to hold her breath for longer and longer distances. When she protested, the coach explained that he was trying to get her to be comfortable with being uncomfortable. That phrase stuck with Jackie. She realized that in many ways she was learning to be comfortable with the uncomfortable.

God did not call us to a life of being comfortable. We tend to want to avoid conflict and confrontation. We try to ignore or deny that we need to work on areas of our lives. We live in a society that embraces being comfortable. We are called to be ministers of reconciliation, which takes a lot of work and is often difficult! We are called to freedom and peace, but to get there we have to allow God to extract our anxious thoughts and fears. We are at home with our status quo, but God wants to move us out of our comfort zone into His purpose. When we are in God's will we can expect opposition from the enemy (there's nothing comfortable about that), but we can also know that we are more than conquerors through God's ever-present love.

Jackie next shared how she and Chrissy Young were in a running group called "Team IBProFun." The group is made up of people of all abilities from beginners to very elite runners. Through their interactions, prayers, and talking freely and excitedly about the World Vision race, they began to draw some interest from their IBProFun colleagues. Friendships that were already developing now were intersecting with the work that God was doing. Over time several of the "Team IBProFun" joined the Olive Knoll's team, "Team Bakersfield for Water." A couple of them came to church. One in particular added her cross to our new believer's wall at church and was baptized into a new found faith in Christ a few months ago!

This is organic outreach at its finest. When we begin taking steps to connect regularly with people in our community, we are following the way of Jesus. Being holy as He is holy is not the same as acting "holier than thou." Jesus regularly met with people over a meal, visited with people on the hillsides, spoke and loved the lovely and the unlovely. He didn't shy away from spending time with a diverse cross section of people in his culture and society. "We are called to incarnate God's message of grace by making space in our lives and our schedules and finding ways to connect with people in our communities who are not part of God's family."[3]

Another area Jackie had to stretch and become "uncomfortable" with was giving up her competitive spirit. She sees no problem with trying to improve her time and doing her best. It can actually

[3] Harney, Kevin G. *Organic Outreach for Ordinary People, Sharing Good News Naturally.* Grand Rapids, Michigan: Zondervan, 2009. P. 132

provide more opportunities as she attempts to enter certain events that are meant for the more elite runner. However, as team captain of the World Vision group, Jackie knew she would need to dedicate more of her time to hanging back and supporting those who were at a variety of levels in their running journey. They would need encouragement and prodding to keep running the race and enduring the training.

Our walk with Christ is similar. We need to always be working to improve our relationship with Him, draw closer to Him, and become more like Him. One person may be on a completely different plane of commitment and maturity than another. Just because someone lacks experience, we shouldn't leave them in the dust. Although we should continue making ourselves sharper, we are also called to come alongside others and help them grow in their walk with Jesus.

Jackie's husband, Allen started his relationship with running as part of rehabilitation for his knee. After surgery from an injury, he knew he needed to strengthen his muscles. Prior to this, he did not see the point of running just to run. He was a basketball player at heart, and running up and down the court made sense. Running for distance and time did not compute in his brain as a worthwhile activity. He is now an enthusiastic runner, or at least he has learned to "embrace the pain." He explained, "You hit a wall, you don't think you can go on, but you continue to press on to the goal that is set before you."

Allen told of a time when he first started running. He passed a lady in the first part of the race who was obviously overcoming a disability. He remembered feeling sorry for her as he strode past her. She was seemingly just barely going to make it, dragging her hindered leg along. Later in the race, Allen had hit his wall. He had broken down at mile twelve and did not think he could take another step. About that time, the lady he had seen at mile one passed by. It was apparent that they were all in this together, and no one had a particular advantage over another. We all run the same distance! The ones who are out there longer actually have greater endurance! It's all in the perspective.

As Jackie and Allen continued to reflect on spiritual connections they found with running, they were excited to share about a recent sermon. Two days before, Pastor Darren had shared from 1 Corinthians 9:24-27, where Paul was talking about the Isthmian Games that occurred in Corinth every other year. These foot races that took place were second only to the Olympian Games. Pastor Darren's points were: 1) Resolve to win; 2) Resolve to train; 3) Resolve to be purposeful; 4) Resolve to be disciplined. How perfect for our conversation on this day, connecting our spiritual pursuits with a physical race.

One more thing that blessed my heart was a quite unexpected surprise later that afternoon. Shortly after we had talked, I picked up the mail. There was a small card with a name and return address that I didn't recognize. When I opened it, I realized it was from Jackie's mom. She had lived for a time in Bakersfield, but when she remarried she had moved to Virginia with her husband. Her name change is what had thrown me off. She was thanking me for *Common Ground.* Jackie had sent her a copy, and she was going through it a second time with her husband. What an act of encouragement! She was running the race and cheering others to keep striving for the true prize!

Soil-Sifting Summary

- When God is in the plans, He goes ahead of us and prepares the path.
- God did not call us to a life of being comfortable, but to a life of reconciliation and purpose.
- When we are in God's will we can expect opposition from the enemy (there's nothing comfortable about that), but we can also know that we are more than conquerors through God's ever-present love.
- When we begin taking steps to connect regularly with people in our community, we are following the way of Jesus.
- We are to continue making ourselves sharper, but we are also called to come alongside others and help them grow in their walk with Jesus.
- When you hit a wall, and you don't think you can go on, continue to press on to the goal that is set before you.
- 1) Resolve to win; 2) Resolve to train; 3) Resolve to be purposeful; 4) Resolve to be disciplined.

Digging into God's Word

- Proverbs 16:9
- 2 Corinthians 5:17-21
- Romans 8:35-39
- Philippians 2:6-7
- Proverbs 27:17
- Philippians 3:12-14
- 1 Corinthians 9:24-27

Extracting Truths and Treasures

Chapter 20
OUT OF THE MIRE

He lifted me out of the slimy pit, out of the mud and mire; he set my feet on a rock and gave me a firm place to stand. Psalm 40:2

When my oldest two boys were two and a half and four years old, they were playing in the backyard of our home. I could hear and see them through the open patio door. It was a warm day, and I was letting them play with the hose. I was enjoying hearing their laughter and squeals, taking in the innocence of their lives and the pleasure they were experiencing over something as simple as a small trickle of water on a hot afternoon. Before long, I noticed the noise had diminished. Any mom knows that silence isn't necessarily golden when it comes to their kids, so I decided I'd better check out the mischief. I walked to the door to get a better look at what was taking place. The water had mixed with the soil in a perfect mixture of thick mud. They were "painting" each other from head to foot with black goop. I let them continue for a few minutes before calling them over to get cleaned up. I tried to keep a straight face as I looked at their little eyes peeking through their mud-clad faces. It was quite adorable, but I didn't want to encourage this type of activity on a regular basis. I later penned this poem:

Beauty in the Mud

Is there beauty in the mud?
There is when it's covering two precious boys head to foot.
That mud!

Without which we couldn't have the grass for which we have so longed;
That mud!
With its rich minerals and moisture—and God's loving care—
Causes things to grow and beautify our world.
So as the two mud clowns shuffle sheepishly onto the patio for their
shower,
I try to hide my smile as I think...
Yes, there's beauty in the mud.

Jan Unfried
January 27, 1985

Of course, this picture-worthy mud bath was cute. Our lives, however, can get pretty ugly and stained as we try to tromp through the mire of sin and hardship. We get deeper and deeper into a pit, and Satan is happy to keep us there. Joyce Meyers says, "He [Satan] is always trying to throw us into pits because he knows that's where he's headed. He's throwing a fit on the way to the pit."[4] The sides are slimy, and as we desperately attempt to climb out, we just slip right back down to the bottom. The swampy, boggy ground makes it impossible for us to even take a step. Each effort at moving forward is rewarded with mud that sticks to our shoes. Then more mud sticks to that and continues to compound, with the hopeless result of great balls of congealed glop surrounding our feet. The weight becomes more than we can maneuver, and we end up sitting down in the middle of the pit, filled with despair, seeing no way up or out.

---

4 *Everyday Answers with Joyce Meyers.* "How to Get Out of the Pit You're In!". Meyers, Joyce. https://joycemeyer.org/everydayanswers/ea-teachings/how-to-get-out-of-the-pit-you-are-in

There are many places in scripture where we are given a command to action. God wants us to follow and obey Him, doing what His Word says. In the case of the pit, however, we are helpless to perform. As we cry out to God, He hears us! He then does the heavy lifting. He pulls us out, sets our feet on a rock, and gives us a firm place to stand. Once we are on the rock, and before taking another step of faith, He turns his cleansing stream of forgiveness on us so that our slime-laden feet don't cause us to fall back into the pit. He cleanses us from our sins and puts a new song in our hearts. This is not anything we can do on our own! It only comes through His grace and mercy!

Jen Rush has accepted God's grace and mercy! Her story of being brought out of the miry clay is amazing, and the new song in her heart is encouraging and inspiring. For all her life, Jen knew and understood pain. From the time she was born, she can remember suffering with migraines. Her earliest memories were of being allowed to lay on an isolated cot in preschool because the noise, lights, and smells were too much for her. Through elementary grades, she continued to experience headaches. Doctors treated her with medication, but never really looked for a root cause.

As puberty hit, the migraines became more frequent and intense. The doctor kept adding medications as a solution. Included in her entourage of prescriptions were pain pills, muscle relaxers, and anti-depression drugs. The effects of all of these medications left her sluggish and ill-equipped to attend classes. She ended up being home schooled to complete her diploma. However, the main lesson she learned throughout high school was, "If you don't feel right, pop a pill."

Jen struggled with why God would allow her to experience such great pain. She had grown up attending church with her grandma. She went to Our Lady of Perpetual Help School in first through fourth grade, receiving religious training along with her studies. She gave her heart to Jesus when she was thirteen years old. She prayed to God and attempted to live for Him. It was probably her knowledge that God would not approve of suicide that was about the only thing that kept her from attempting to take her own life when her physical pain was excruciating.

After high school and two failed marriages, Jen was in a relationship for 16 years. During that time she went through ten surgeries and two automobile accidents. She became so familiar with hospital and paramedic staff that she knew the doctors, nurses, and ambulance drivers by name. Through all of this time, she felt increasingly less supported emotionally by her boyfriend. She was thrown into a deep depression between 2015 and 2018. She was taking Norco, a prescription medication that combines hydrocodone with acetaminophen, regularly and in higher doses daily.

In the summer of 2018, her mom was diagnosed with cancer. Jen went to her parents' home to help take care of her mom. Still suffering from depression and pain herself, Jen continued to seek professional care for relief. In November of 2018, she was prescribed Latuda, an antipsychotic used to treat schizophrenia. As a reaction to the medicine, she began hearing voices. They were telling her that her family didn't want her, that she was the worst person, and that she didn't deserve to live. Accompanying these auditory hallucinations was an excruciating migraine that lasted for thirty days.

Not thinking clearly and enduring unbearable pain, Jen went into a rage. She began to destroy her parents' home, and in the ensuing chaos her parents were physically hurt. They loved Jen, and she loved them. She had no intention of hurting them, but they also knew they were helpless in that moment to calm her down. After they tried in vain to get the psychiatric facility to come and get her, their only recourse, for their own safety, was to call the police. Jen was charged with a felon because she had caused harm to individuals over sixty-five years of age. She was placed in the mental health ward of the downtown jail for three days.

It was in this pit of despair that Jen cried out to God. She begged Him to help her through this and to take away her pain. She grieved over the pain she was causing to those she loved. She poured out her heart to God and promised to give God her life, to give Him everything. From that moment forward, Jen kept her promise! God lifted her out of the pit and placed her on **solid ground.** Even the time in jail was being used to continue the cleansing of her mud-caked feet and ensure that there was no slippery slime clinging to her to cause her to slide back.

Upon being transferred to the Lerdo Detention Facility, the first thing Jen did was to grab a Bible. She read Psalm 38 over and over again. With King David, Jen was asking the Lord to not forsake her and to come quickly to help her. She poured over the Scripture in her cell, with other inmates who would read with her, and she kept praying for God to go before her. God did not abandon nor forsake her! He helped her to be assigned just the right public defender who helped expedite her time of incarceration to a mere ten days. Jen suffered mild withdrawal symptoms while in jail, but was freed from her horrendous pain. Her shoulder, which had limited movement due to an accident, was completely restored. Her headaches dissipated, and her mind cleared from being off the medications and from being renewed by God's Word.

Getting out of jail is not an easy thing. Yes, Jen was no longer behind bars, but now she was homeless. There was a restraining order against her, so she could not go near her parents. Wanting to do things legally, she contacted the police department to take her to get her car, keys, and wallet. For the next few days, leading up to Christmas, she lived in her car, stayed with a friend for a couple of nights, and procured a bed in a shelter. In the meantime, she immersed herself in any and every church service and Bible study that she could find. She was relying completely and solely on God for every decision and every move she made. She knew she didn't want to ever go back to pills to help her through life.

Two days before Christmas, an opportunity arose for Jen to pay rent to stay in an extra room a lady had at her house. From December 23, 2018, to March 2019, she stayed there. She continued to immerse herself in God. She discovered Celebrate Recovery (CR) at Olive Knolls and felt immediately at home. During a discussion and prayer with one of the other CR participants, Jen applied and was accepted to live at the Keeper's Transformation House. This enabled her to save on gas, as she could now walk to Bible studies and several of the weekly services.

Jen continues to seek God for direction and has waited on His timing and His clear guidance. As a result, she has a place to live and a new car. She has been able to reconcile with her parents, her daughter, son-in-law, and granddaughter. She has a new purpose and is seeking a potential career in teaching God's Word. Jen has a new song—a song of praise to her God and King! I don't know if there is beauty **in** the mud, but I know God can bring growth and beauty out of the mud. Jen is a striking example of being lifted out of the mire and claiming His glorious work and miracles!

Soil-Sifting Summary

- When we are in the pit, God does the heavy lifting. He pulls us out, sets our feet on a rock, gives us a firm place to stand, and puts a new song in our hearts.
- God's cleansing of our sins is not anything we can do on our own! It only comes through His grace and mercy!
- When we cry out to God, ask His forgiveness, and seek Him, He is faithful to answer us!
- Like King David, we can be honest and open in our confession and cries for help.
- God is faithful to His promise to never leave nor forsake us.
- God's healing includes freeing us from the pit, healing our diseases, and renewing our minds.
- God gives us a new song of victory that will bring glory to His name and encourage others who hear of his mighty works.

Digging into God's Word

- Psalm 40:1-3
- Ephesians 2:4-10
- 1 John 1:8-9
- Psalm 38
- Deuteronomy 31:6
- Psalm 103:1-5
- Psalm 98

Extracting Truths and Treasures

Christ,
Our Firm
Foundation

Chapter 21

WHEN GOD STIRS

So the Lord stirred up the spirit of Zerubbabel son of Shealtiel, governor of Judah, and the spirit of Joshua son of Jehozadak, the high priest, and the spirit of the whole remnant of the people. They came and began to work on the house of the Lord Almighty, their God. Haggai 1:14

In the 1930's there was a phenomenon known as the Dust Bowl. The American and Canadian prairies were experiencing a wide-spread drought. In addition, the farmers' failed to apply dryland farming methods which would prevent wind erosion. As prevailing prairie winds came through, the unanchored dust stirred up in great clouds, sometimes called "black blizzards," as they would darken the sky and block out the sun.

Between 1930 and 1940 a mass exodus of families began from Texas, Oklahoma, and the surrounding Great Plains. People had lost their homes and their livelihoods, and there did not seem to be an end in sight. It is estimated that approximately 3.5 million people migrated from the Plains states during this time. The dismal state of these families, who left everything behind, was exacerbated by the Great Depression during the 1930's.

John Knox's family was part of the "Okies" that headed to California with five kids and very few possessions in their Ford Model T Coupe. Another motivation for leaving the Midwest was because John, born in 1934, had severe asthma. His respiratory condition was life-threatening for him, and it was only made worse by the humidity and dust he was breathing. The family didn't have money for the treatments he needed, so eventually a judge gave a court order for the hospital to treat him. The doctor made an immediate decision that the only way John would survive would be to move to a more suitable climate.

They made their way to California, stopping on the side of the road at night to throw their blankets on the ground to sleep. Once in California, his parents followed the seasonal crops between the Imperial Valley and the Central Valley. The work was hard, the living conditions temporary and less than ideal. Their family eventually landed in Wasco, California, in a labor camp. They lived in a tent cabin. Their dad would string wire across the room so they could hang blankets and create separations between sleeping areas. Their only bathrooms were the outhouses, and running water was absent.

John's earliest recollection was picking cotton with his mom when he was about four years old. Everyone helped, so he would accompany her as she walked down the row of cotton, grasping the cotton balls and twisting them off of the boll. He would walk in front of her and make little piles for her to pick up and place into her bag. When John got tired, she would tamp down the cotton, place him inside the bag, and drag him along as she continued to harvest her portion. He would get a nice little nap in this soft, padded, make-shift bed.

John started school in Wasco at age five. He continued to join his mom after school and on Saturdays in the cotton fields. Everything shut down on Sundays for a day of rest. Eventually his family began attending the Assembly of God Church in town. When John entered his teen years, their church didn't have much of a youth group. It consisted of only John and one other guy who was four years older than him. Starting his junior year in high school, he got permission from his dad to go to the Nazarene church, which had a pretty good sized teen group. His older sister and one of his brothers were already attending the Nazarene church, so his dad allowed John to attend.

One of the friends John met was Donna. She was a couple years younger than him, but they immediately clicked. Donna's family had also migrated from Oklahoma during the Dust Bowl. Her dad was set to start a job in Kansas, but at the last minute he received a telegram that the job was no longer available. Since they had family members in Wasco, her dad headed to California to look for work. When Donna's sister was six weeks old and Donna was five, her mom received money from her dad to get on the train and join him. Donna can remember soldiers helping her mother on and off the train with the little ones.

Donna's family lived in a little cabin that was grouped in an area owned by a "bunch" of their relatives. Everyone worked the crops, picking cotton, grapes, potatoes, and whatever was in season at the time. Her dad ended up working at a service station. He eventually took over and owned the station. They had a home that was always open to guests, and there was always extra room at the table. As they got into their teen years, many times Donna's younger sister would invite some of the basketball players over. She would then come home and give Donna the responsibility of making homemade ice cream to be ready upon the team members' arrival. During Donna's early years in Wasco, her parents did not attend church, but she and her sister faithfully attended. The church became their extended family. God was stirring her spirit at a young age to build His kingdom.

God was also stirring John's spirit. At age fifteen, the youth pastor, Gabe Martinez, led John to the Lord. John recognized this as a huge pivotal moment in his life. Prior to asking Jesus into his life, John described himself as a bashful kid with a slight stutter. After meeting Jesus, John became bold in his faith. He and some friends started a Bible club at school called the CLOC Club (Christians Living on Campus). He was the president of this club. On the basketball team, John was the sixth man on the team and was sitting on the bench a good portion of the games. After three of the star players were kicked off the team due to being caught with alcohol, John became a starter and a leader on the team. At the end of a really tough loss, the coach asked John to pray for the team. From then on he prayed before each game with the team. He had no trouble sharing Jesus with others. John became the MVP of the team. He said that his leadership role was not as much about his playing ability as it was about the confidence that God had instilled in him.

John went off to Pasadena College. During his senior year, Donna came to the same college as a freshman. He describes their relationship as being "friends, friends, friends." I think Donna might have hoped for a little more. They finally began to date after John graduated and Donna was in her sophomore year. They were engaged in August of 1957, but the only way Donna's dad would agree was if they promised that Donna would finish college. John was drafted in September of 1957, and they were married while he was in boot camp in December of that year. While serving in Germany, Donna contacted him through the Red Cross to let him know that his dad was dying. John came home and was able to see his dad just before he passed. During this short stint at home, Donna became pregnant. John returned to Germany, Donna graduated "magna cum baby" in May, and their first child was born in July.

When John finished his military duty and came home in August, they began figuring out their future. Donna got a teaching job in Glendora while John coached basketball with the intention of getting his teaching credential. God provided an amazing babysitter for their new baby girl. The caregiver loved and treated her as one of her own, and Donna felt very comfortable leaving her each day. When John realized that teaching and coaching was not for him, they moved to Fresno. John started in the insurance business there, and they had their second child. They were transferred to San Luis Obispo for a year where baby number three was born. From there they were transferred to Oakland. They were not happy there, so when the opportunity arose to take a job in Bakersfield, John snatched it up. Their fourth child was born in Wasco, just as they were getting ready to move.

Donna had gone ahead of John before the baby was born, and she found a house for the family in Bakersfield. That house never felt like home, and Donna would strongly advise against buying a home while you are pregnant. Eventually they found a perfect home in an area called Green Acres. It needed some TLC, but they settled in and created an open environment for anyone who needed a meal or a cup of coffee or a glass of sun tea. God brought John and Donna together with their unique strengths and united them in their desire to create a godly home and family.

One of the traditions they started was to have an "Open House" every New Year's Eve. Families of all ages would head over to share in food, fun, and fellowship to welcome in the new year. I remember feeling so loved and accepted by the Knox's. They were teaching the young married class at the time we moved to Bakersfield in 1980, and as we were starting our little family, we were receiving great modeling and nurturing.

No matter where they lived, John was always involved in teaching a Sunday school class or Bible study. Over the years he has worked with teens, young married couples, senior adults, a surfers' group, men's Bible studies, and many others. He has ministered in convalescent homes, rescue missions, and hospitals. He joked about the fact that the only class he failed in college was his Bible class. His credentials for leading these classes was a life with Jesus and pouring himself into studying God's Word. He also realized the importance of relationship building, living life with people.

John declared that their life has been surrounded by the church and serving the Lord. They didn't wait for others to invite them in. Instead they set about providing a place of hospitality for others. When they moved to their current location in Cayucos, John was teaching a class of about forty people on Rick Warren's book, *The Purpose Driven Life*. They began having groups of ten to twelve people over each Sunday for lunch, and once again they became rooted deeply in the lives of others. They had people who actually teared up because they had never been invited into someone's home, and they were hungry for and thrilled to have this fellowship.

Donna began cooking Thursday lunch once a month at the church for John's men's Bible study group. The men so thoroughly enjoyed the meal and fellowship, that John and Donna were approached by the pastor about expanding it to the 55+ age group once a month. Eventually, it became known as the "Lunch Bunch" which was open to anyone, any age group, at no charge. As many as seventy people would show up on a given Thursday at noon. John reflected, "You find out more about people sitting over the dinner table talking." It is amazing how people crave relationships and being together.

One of the things that struck me as we concluded our conversation was that John spoke about his current ministry and purpose God has given him as the best in all of his years. You must realize by now, that John and Donna are in their eighties. God is not finished with them yet. John gets such encouragement and inspiration from visiting people in the hospital and occasionally being able to lead a non-believer to Christ. A group that meets for coffee on Friday morning at McDonald's prayed one morning with a lady who seemed to be down and out. She shared that her son was in Oklahoma, dying of cancer. She didn't have the means to visit him, and she was certain he would die before she saw him again. They prayed for his healing, and for his wife and little child.

Three of the men from this group, including John, felt an urgency to take their faith into action. They wrote a check for a plane ticket for her to go back to see her son. With tears in her eyes, she couldn't believe anyone would care about her that much. They shared with her that there is Someone who loves her more than them! She prayed the sinner's prayer and received Christ. She was immediately concerned about her son not knowing the Lord, especially with death at his door. The men were able to make contact with a local pastor who went to the son's house. He led the man and his wife to the Lord. The son's cancer went into remission, and he and his wife are serving God in Oklahoma.

What an interesting circling back. God stirred the dust in Oklahoma to get John and Donna's families to move to California.

There, in His providence and timing, their hearts were stirred to surrender to the Lord, and He established them on **solid ground**. John and Donna met and continued to build God's house and the kingdom. As they continued to be obedient, God stirred the hearts of the men in McDonald's to pray for and lead a new sheep into the fold. The stirring made its way back to Oklahoma as God provided a miracle of physical and spiritual healing in the lives of another family. Who knows how many more will enter Heaven because of the ripple effect of lives committed to Him.

Soil–Sifting Summary

- After meeting Jesus, John went from being a bashful young teen to someone bold in his faith. This reminds us that when we come to Christ, we are a new creation!
- Relationship building is such an important part of living life with others. Hospitality was a natural part of John and Donna's life.
- "You find out more about people sitting over the dinner table talking." It is amazing how people crave relationship and being together.
- John and Donna are in their eighties. God is not finished with them yet.
- In God's providence and timing, John and Donna's hearts were stirred to surrender to the Lord, and He established them on **solid ground**. They have served Him ever since, and are continuing to work on the "house of the Lord Almighty, their God."

Digging into God's Word

- 2 Corinthians 5:17
- 1 Peter 4:8–9
- Acts 2:42–47
- Philippians 1:6
- Haggai 1:14

Extracting Truths and Treasures

Chapter 22
A NEW HEART

I will give you a new heart and put a new spirit in you; I will
remove from you your heart of stone and give you a heart of flesh.
Ezekiel 36:26

$\mathcal{M}$arie Kondo is world renowned for her advice on
organizing and tidying up your home. She helps others
declutter their closets and drawers with step-by-step tips and
illustrated books. Going through your house by category (clothes,
books, papers, etc.), Kondo suggests if an item no longer brings you
joy, discard it. Let it go!

During our remodel I had two opportunities to do some major
decluttering. First, we packed everything in boxes and stored them
in our garage. As I was pulling things out from the back of cabinets
and drawers, I had no trouble letting go of a lot of it. We sold some
of our "stuff" at a big garage sale. We took some of our things to
local nonprofit organizations so our gently used home goods could
hopefully find a new home. We threw away bags of unnecessary
junk that had somehow crept its way into special dark spaces that
had not seen the light of day for many years.

This purging felt liberating. Then, it came time to put things
back into the newly renovated spaces. More and more things could
not pass the "sparks joy" test. We placed some things on the
Internet to sell (I wasn't going to have another garage sale!), gave
more away, and filled a few more garbage bags. I'm not saying I

have a Kondo-approved house, but my cupboards and closets are much less cluttered. I even have a few empty spaces that I am not looking to fill any time soon.

Just as we tend to hold onto excess and unneeded items in our homes, we also tend to hold onto pointless things in our lives. We know these things are not bringing us joy. We know we should let them go. We stuff them into the dark recesses of our hearts and minds and pretend like they aren't there. Then we hear a sermon, attend a class, or read a passage of scripture that exposes our hidden "junk." We are faced with the choice of harboring the things that are keeping us enslaved or giving them to the One who can free us.

My friend, Joyce, shared with me about the freedom she had experienced because of choosing to be obedient to Jesus' call on her life to give up a concealed unforgiving attitude. Joyce's story in my book, *Common Ground* ("A Heartbeat for God"), told about how she had learned to give up her control issues. Not only did she get a physical healing for her heart, but she received spiritual victory and rest. Now it was time for her to take on another heart-cleansing task.

Joyce was participating in a Biblical study called "Courageous Hearts." The curriculum is designed to help people with eating disorders. Joyce had always thought that her problem with overeating was because of some weakness she had. She was learning that her relationship with food had replaced a healthy and full relationship with God. The group was working through various areas in their lives that would help reverse that trend. One of the week's lessons during this study was on forgiveness. The class members had to write down the names of those who they had a hard time forgiving. Joyce felt like she had done a pretty good job with forgiving. She realized how important it was. She had always heard that "when you don't forgive, it's like you are taking poison and expecting the other person to die." With this knowledge, she had kept forgiveness at the forefront of her relationships, so her list was not too extensive.

There was **one** person that Joyce had attempted to give to the Lord. It was someone she had once held dear, but who had hurt her deeply during a very troubling time. Joyce would relinquish her to the Lord in one moment, but in the next moment she would pick her back up and drag her around. Joyce described it like a millstone around her neck. The weight of no longer being able to love this person was a heavy burden. Joyce admitted not just "thinking" hurtful things about her, but also saying hurtful things to others about her. In the world's eyes, Joyce was justified. How could she forgive the wife, now ex-wife, of her dying son? Her daughter-in-law had left her son when he was in a vulnerable place physically and emotionally, and Joyce just couldn't let go of her own anger and pain.

The physical weight we feel when we are not living in God's will is real. God wants to give us a new heart and take away our heart of stone. A heart of stone indicates hardness and heaviness. He wants to put a new spirit in us and renew us. It is only something God can do, but we have to be honest and open and willing to do some hard work. We have to allow God to expose those deep dark places and admit we are powerless on our own to "tidy" them up.

The exercise for the students in the class was to write down the sentence, "I forgive _____, but..." They were to keep writing this phrase putting the person's name in the blank until they ran out of "buts." Joyce had four pages of detailed and precise declarations following this sentence pattern. Over the next few weeks she was to take each individual "but" and give it to God. One at a time, slowly, prayerfully, she handed each painful issue to God. She felt like the millstone was crumbling. The burden was feeling lighter and smaller with each surrender, until she felt totally released from the oppression of carrying this nasty, horrible unforgiving feeling. She was so grateful and gave the glory and praise to God.

Then came the test! Joyce's father was hospitalized in December, where he was receiving respiratory therapy each day for three or four hours. One day while Joyce was sitting with her dad, a young nurse came into the room. Her dad was napping and the room was dark. The young lady was wearing a mask, and she made it a point not to introduce herself. This nurse knew the person she was servicing. She also knew Joyce, and she was aware of the painful rift in their relationship. She wanted to just do her job and leave. She shared later that she had been afraid to come up to this room!

To keep things professional, she went over to the patient to let him know she was there to do his respiratory therapy. The patient, Joyce's dad, opened his eyes and said, "Aren't you my granddaughter?" At this point, Joyce spoke to her and recognized her as well. It was her ex-daughter-in law, the one she had worked so hard to forgive. Now she was seeing her face-to-face. Joyce shared, "Miracle of miracles! All the love just flowed into me." She had an immense love for her and it was like it used to be. They caught up on life, and Joyce was able to speak encouragement into her life. She let her know how proud she was of her for pursuing her career. God proved Himself faithful by filling Joyce and the room with His love and presence. Instead of feeling shaken by the encounter, Joyce felt like she was standing on the **solid ground** of God's mercy and grace.

Joyce learned a valuable lesson! Her job was not to try to figure out why other people acted the way they did or to rationalize her disappointment when they didn't meet her expectations. Her job was to forgive, so God could continue to work in her life. To love as Christ loved us and to forgive as He forgave us is such an important key to living a life of freedom!

God's Word is our manual on how to tidy up our hearts. The Scriptures penetrate our thoughts and attitudes. His commands, declarations, and promises are useful for teaching and rebuking, correcting and training. The Bible equips us for every good work. When we sold our yard-sale items, we didn't get back their worth in market value. The amazing thing with God is that when we give Him our "junk," we definitely trade up. He takes the things that are causing us pain and sorrow and gives us His joy and peace. He doesn't just organize and declutter. He creates a new heart!

Soil-Sifting Summary

- We are sometimes faced with the choice of harboring the things that are keeping us enslaved OR giving them to the One who can free us.
- Holding onto an unforgiving attitude creates a heavy burden, but when it is given to God our burdens are lifted.
- God wants to give us a new heart and take away our heart of stone.
- To love as Christ loved us and to forgive as He forgave us is such an important key to living a life of freedom!
- God's Word is our manual on how to tidy up our hearts. The Scriptures penetrate our thoughts and attitudes. His commands, declarations, and promises are useful for teaching and rebuking, correcting and training. The Bible equips us for every good work.

Digging into God's Word

- Deuteronomy 30:19-20
- Psalm 38:4
- Matthew 11:28-30
- Ezekiel 36:25-27
- Colossians 3:13
- Hebrews 4:12
- 2 Timothy 3:16-17

Extracting Truths and Treasures

Chapter 23
SEVENTH FLOOR FIASCO

He who dwells in the shelter of the Most High will rest in the shadow of the Almighty. Psalm 91:1

On a recent trip to Baltimore, some crazy things occurred. My husband and I were going to do grandparent duty with our nine month old grandson while our daughter-in-law attended a four-day math conference. My sister calls me the "Granny Nanny" because I rarely will turn down an opportunity to watch one or more of my grandkids! This was a city we had not been to in previous travels, so we were excited to do some exploring within the confines of having a baby in a stroller.

Baltimore, Maryland, is the largest city in the state. Our hotel was located in the city's Inner Harbor. We were able to walk through Oriole's stadium and Camden Yard. Not far from the Oriole's baseball home, we toured Babe Ruth's Birthplace and Museum. This legendary figure had a big personality to match his record-setting homeruns. Next we hit a grand slam as we viewed the beautiful cityscape from the Top of the World Observation Level of the Baltimore World Trade Center. A collection of warships, including the historic USS Constellation, was docked below.

Before we had the opportunity to discover these sites, we had to make it through our first twenty-four hours. Our first catastrophe happened as we arrived at the luggage carousel. The three adults in our party were already juggling the maximum number of carry-ons: two backpacks, a diaper bag, a purse, a computer bag, and a small rolling suitcase. We also had a stroller and car seat that had been checked at the gate, and, of course, we had the baby! Our three larger bags had taken a ride in the bowels of the plane, and we were now watching our flight's' precious cargo being deposited onto the conveyor belt. When everything seemed to be claimed on this merry-go-round of people's paraphernalia, we had only retrieved two of our three suitcases.

I had prayed earlier in the day for God to give me a chance to count on Him to live out the fruit of the Spirit: Peace, patience, kindness, self-control, etc. You must be careful how you pray! God was giving me a perfect occasion to put His Word into action. It was my bag that had been "misplaced." I took a deep breath before speaking to the claims office. The lady who helped me was also named Janice, so we were off to a good start. The Baltimore Southwest terminal had experienced a four-hour computer shut down earlier in the day caused by a news-worthy glitch with a data streaming vendor. This knowledge helped me to have a little empathy for the employees.

With as much kindness and patience as I could muster, I filled out all the necessary paperwork. I gathered my incident report and the rest of my crew, and we finally made it to our hotel. I began to feel a little giddy as I prided myself in my attitude. I was enjoying an imaginary shopping trip to buy some new clothes for the trip. Alas, I received an email shortly after midnight from DeliveryInfo@wheresmysuitcase.com (I am not making this up!). They were letting me know my luggage had been delivered at the front desk of our hotel. So instead of a shopping spree, I humbly went down the next morning to retrieve my redeemed baggage.

The next crisis that we faced was a sick baby. Whether he had caught a bug or had eaten something that disagreed with him, our little guy started throwing up about 1:30 AM. It was still just our first night! We had to call for clean blankets and sheets for the crib as well as extra towels, since we had used several to clean things up. After a couple bouts of emptying his stomach, he seemed to settle down. He actually slept until 9:00 AM. Since he seemed to be feeling better, his mom decided to nurse him when he awoke. Shortly after downing his breakfast, he vomited the entire intake all over his mother's bed. Fortunately, that was the last of the spewing incidents, but we now needed a complete change of her bedding.

Our daughter-in-law deemed that the baby was going to be okay, and she trusted we could handle things. After skipping the first couple of sessions, she went off to her conference. Attempting to prove that we were competent, we had called the front desk to request housekeeping to change the sheets as soon as possible. The morning went by and we had no service. Early in the afternoon, we made our second request. We had actually seen the service cart in the hallway. My husband even spoke to the employee and let them know it was a great time to service our room because the baby was in between naps. Even with all of our proactive exploits, for some reason the maid completely skipped our room. At second glance, the cart was gone, the hallway was empty. We made our third plea. By now it was about 5:00 PM and the housekeeping staff had gone home for the day. Explaining that we were just short of coming down and getting the sheets for ourselves, I think the staff finally realized our desperation. About 5:30 PM a harried lady arrived at our seventh floor room.

She was visibly and verbally upset. She was supposed to be ending her day and going home when she was summoned to take care of our issue. She couldn't understand why it hadn't been handled in the routine servicing of the room earlier that day. We couldn't have agreed with her more. We realized that returning our frustration for her anger would be non-productive. She needed some understanding and empathy. My husband greeted her with kindness and thanked her so much for coming to our aid. He then left to get some dinner, while I stayed in the room with our little guy. I continued to talk with our helper, showing genuine interest in her life and letting her know how bad we felt that she had to delay the end of her work day for us.

Charlotte's story eventually came spilling out. Our mutual connection of having grandchildren got her talking about her own grandkids and her own children. I found out her nineteen year-old son had been murdered in the streets of Baltimore. He had been with the wrong person at the wrong time, and a bullet meant for the other guy had found her son as its target. A few months later she lost a grandchild. Though the details weren't shared, you could tell she was still raw from the grief and pain.

Charlotte told me that she had a faith in God. It helped her to know that He needed her "angels" in Heaven more than she needed them on Earth. Even with that outlook, it had taken a great toll on her life. She had been a practicing nurse, but had given up her job. It was just too hard to see injured patients come into her ward without reliving her own personal, tragic moments. Now she was performing manual labor at a fraction of the previous income she had earned, just to get by.

My heart broke for Charlotte. I told her I didn't think it was a coincidence that she was the one sent up to take care of our seventh floor fiasco. I believed we were supposed to meet and that she was supposed to share her story with me. Soon Charlotte's attitude and demeanor changed. Before she left, I prayed with her. I thanked God for sending her up to our room and allowing our encounter to take place. I asked God to bless her life and her work and her heart. I prayed for her pain and grief. She agreed with me in prayer with "uh-huhs," and "mmm's." When we opened our eyes, we both had tears and we embraced in a hug.

You see, that's how God is. He takes our fiascos and turns them into blessings. Just as my lost luggage was found, Jesus finds lives that were once lost, and He miraculously changes them in His mercy and grace. Our room was finally serviced...FINALLY. Yet how much more our patient waiting on the good timing of God will result in amazing and surprising benefits. A disgruntled employee had a change of heart. How much more God wants to take our hearts' anguish and turn it into joy. We will all have trouble in this life. It comes with the territory! It comes in a variety of shapes and sizes, extents and intensities. But we can take heart. It's only in Christ that we can receive peace because He has overcome the world!

Our seventh floor disasters brought us to the **solid ground** floor of our foundation in Christ. I couldn't take away the pain for Charlotte, but the abiding Rock could provide a dwelling place for her and allow her to rest in the shadow of the Almighty.

Soil-Sifting Summary

- When we pray for the fruit of the Spirit to be manifested in our lives, we should be ready to practice His goodness.
- Returning frustration and annoyance for the anger and resentment of someone else is non-productive.
- We can take heart. It's only in Christ that we can receive peace because He has overcome the world!
- Through our trials we can abide in God. He is our abiding Rock who provides a dwelling place. He allows us to rest in His shadow.

Digging into God's Word

- Galatians 5:22-23
- Proverbs 15:1
- John 16:33
- Psalm 91:1-4

Extracting Truths and Treasures

Chapter 24

OUR CORNERSTONE

So this is what the Sovereign Lord says: "See, I lay a stone in Zion, a tested stone, a precious cornerstone for a sure foundation; the one who trusts will never be dismayed." Isaiah 28:16

𝒯he Old Testament has many references to altars. Countless times, Biblical characters took a moment to build an altar to remember a significant event and to worship their God. In the book of Genesis, Noah built an altar to the Lord when they were finally able to exit the ark onto dry ground. Abram and Isaac built altars at Shechem, Hebron, and Beersheba in response to God's promises to them and their offspring. Later, in the book of Exodus, Moses built an altar after God had brought an important victory to the Israelites. Moses called this place "The Lord is my Banner."

The altar building continued in the book of Joshua. Joshua set up his altar with twelve stones, each picked up from the middle of the Jordan River and carried by a man from one of the twelve tribes of Israel. This twelve-stone memorial was to be a reminder of when the flow of the Jordan was cut off before the ark of the covenant of the Lord so that the people could cross. Later, at a place called Mount Ebal, Joshua built an altar to the Lord for burnt offerings and fellowship offerings.

In the book of Judges, Gideon built an altar in response to God's call on his life and God's promise of peace. He called it "The Lord is

Peace." Samuel's stone in 1 Samuel was called Ebenezer, meaning "Thus far the Lord has helped us." Moving through 1 and 2 Samuel and 1 and 2 Kings, King Saul and King David built altars in response to and as an atonement for the nation's sins. The prophet Elijah's altar was prepared to show the power of God and bring revival on the land. Continuing through 1 and 2 Chronicles, Solomon and Asa used altars as acts of obedience and reformation. Hezekiah and Manasseh prepared the altar of the Lord as undertakings of restoration, thanksgiving, consecration, and purification. In the book of Ezra, the priests, Joshua and Zerubbabel, rebuilt the altar as a witness to God delivering His people from exile.

Altars in churches today are equally as important as those in Old Testament times. Since Jesus paid the ultimate once-for-all sacrifice for our sins through His death on the cross, the only sacrifice we need to bring to God is ourselves. As we kneel at an altar of prayer, we come for a variety of purposes, similar to those of our forefathers. We accept Christ's atonement for our sins. We thank God for His provision, protection, and victory. We consecrate and purify our hearts and lives for God's purpose. We pray for and experience revival and restoration.

As we walk with God, we can build altars symbolically or metaphorically. By keeping a picture of a meaningful God-event, journaling a noteworthy moment of God's provision, or marking a significant life-altering date on the calendar, we are creating a "place" to come back to in order to revel in God's faithfulness. Some, like Keith and Don in "Horn of Salvation," build a physical structure to dedicate their life and future to God. The purposes and functions of our altars are personal and unique.

One such special altar is located just off the fire road that Southern California Edison (SCE) created to maintain their power lines. Among those huge towers that look like creatures in a Star Wars movie, is a pile of rocks. It is in the foothills above my brother, Jim's, home in Alta Loma. It's enough off of the road that it is not easy to notice, but if you happen by his path you will find it is lined with stones that lead to his altar.

In 1998 Jim experienced a turning point in his personal spiritual journey and disciplines. He never had an interest in joining a gym, but he loved getting out in the hills around where he lives. He walked, ran, or rode his mountain bike. To make the most of his time, he began combining his time for exercise and prayer.

When Jim and his wife moved to their current location in 2002, he was contemplating some of the scriptures about altars. He had been intentionally reading through the Bible and recognized that altars were a big part of God's people and servants. As he was in the hills for his daily "pray and play," he began to notice how many rocks were exposed and available on his daily walks and rides. One day he felt inspired to build his own altar.

As he prayed about decisions to be made and interceded for people and the problems or situations they had shared with him, or as he sought direction from God, he would associate those things with a stone. Stones were gathered that represented his family members, friends, work associates, his boss, obstacles, death of loved ones, healings, God's amazing provision and milestone accomplishments.

Many of the stones he stacked up have been significant enough in size that he was not able to lift them. He would typically roll them and use leverage from the other stacked stones to hoist them into place. It was a conviction that moving a stone needed to require effort. He moved many from significant distances because they represented heavy burdens.

As we look at the significance of Biblical altars, we find four main purposes for creating them. One of the objectives of altars was to make sacrifices to God (see Genesis 8:20 and Joshua 8:30-31). Jim wanted us to know that God never asked him to sacrifice his son or any animal on his altar. He did note that he had been tempted a time or two during his son's teenage years to take him up there and tie him to the altar! Of course he refrained. Instead he symbolically laid his son on the altar, and just like with Abraham and Isaac, God provided other ways to deal with those years.

Jim has sacrificed much time at the altar for which he has received much blessing. He believes God pours out His blessings on us continuously. God is the giver of good things and wants to bless us at all times so that we can continue to be successful and useful for Him.

A writer by the name of Jonathan Cahn helped Jim understand why some people are blessed and others are not. Cahn used the illustration of a bucket of water and two cups. One cup was upright and the other upside down. He poured the water out of the bucket onto both cups. He then explained that the one who receives God's blessings is the one with their cup upright. The same blessings are available to all, but if your cup is upside down, you don't receive the blessings that God is pouring out.

Jim keeps going back to his altar because he consistently receives God's blessings there. It is a place he can refocus and make sure his cup is turned upright. The stones from all the years remind him of God's goodness and faithfulness and gives him hope for the future.

Another Old Testament purpose of altars was to make atonement for the sins of the people (see Leviticus 16:18-20). Jim has prayed at his altar for many people—family, neighbors and friends—to receive the atonement for their sins that comes from the grace Jesus offers from His sacrifice on the cross. God's grace is available to all who come to Him and believe in His name.

A third purpose for altars was to burn incense to the Lord (see Exodus 30:1-10). The fragrant smoke symbolized the prayers of the people. Jim mentioned that he has never burned incense on his altar, but his altar was burned. In 2003 a wildfire passed through the location. Bulldozers cutting fire lines destroyed his first altar. After grieving his loss he rebuilt it bigger and better. He used a large stone, a foundation stone that he calls his Christ rock. It is on and around this place of **solid ground** that he has stacked all the other stones of remembrance. It has stood the test of time since then.

The final purpose for altars was to function as memorials (see Exodus 17:15 & Joshua 22:26-27). For Jim, this is the main reason he adds a rock to his altar. Each stone has a significant memory attached to it. Some are stones of gratitude for God's clear activity in his life. He admits, that with his old age and the passing of years he wouldn't be able to recall the exact situation or circumstance for each stone's placement. Others, however, are very clear.

The top rock was one he placed in 2011 when our father passed away. It continually reminds Jim that he now has two fathers in heaven... the One Jesus taught us about and the one that taught him about Jesus. For that he is eternally grateful, and visiting his altar regularly helps him to remember he has much to look forward to according to the promise of God. Our future hope is for that great day of reunion and rejoicing in the heavenly home Jesus has gone to prepare for us.

Jim has prayed prayers at this altar declaring his dependence on God. In return, God has blessed him with His peace, power, provision and presence. Jim's testimony is that Jesus is his Cornerstone. All of this is available to you as well. Jim recognizes that not everyone needs an altar in the hills to receive God's blessing. But in order to receive all God wants to give to you, he encourages you to thank God for His blessings and keep your cup upright to accept His abundance. Build your life and trust in Christ, the precious Cornerstone, and you will never be dismayed!

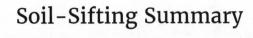

Soil-Sifting Summary

- Altars are referred to all throughout the Old Testament. Countless times Biblical characters took a moment to build an altar to remember a significant event and to worship their God.
- Since Jesus paid the ultimate once-for-all sacrifice for our sins through His death on the cross, the only sacrifice we need to bring to God is ourselves.
- God is the giver of good things and wants to bless us at all times so that we can continue to be successful and useful for Him.
- God's grace is available to all who come to Him and believe in His name.
- Our future hope is for that great day of reunion and rejoicing in the heavenly home Jesus has gone to prepare for us.
- Build your life and trust in Christ, the precious Cornerstone, and you will never be dismayed!

Digging into God's Word

- Genesis 8:20; 12:7-8; 13:18; 26:25
- Genesis 35:6-7
- Exodus 17:15
- Joshua 4:1-9; 8:30-31; Judges 6:24
- 1 Samuel 7:17; 14:35; 2 Samuel 24:25; 1 Kings 18:30-32
- 2 Chronicles 8:12; 15:8; 29:18; 33:16; Ezra 3:2-3
- Romans 12:1; 2 Corinthians 9:8
- Ephesians 2:8-9
- John 14:1-4; Isaiah 28:16

Extracting Truths and Treasures

Chapter 25

THE KEY TO THE

TREASURE

He will be the sure foundation for your times, a rich store of salvation and wisdom and knowledge; the fear of the Lord is the key to this treasure. Isaiah 33:6

There is a beautiful diamond housed at the Smithsonian's Natural History Museum in Washington D.C. The original crudely cut stone, most likely mined from the Kollur mine in Golconda, India, was sold to a merchant in the 1600's. It then made its way through several French kings, was stolen, and eventually purchased and sold by King George IV of the United Kingdom. The Hope Diamond, as it is called, is named for Henry Philip Hope, who procured the diamond in the 1830's. After Mr. Hope's death, this precious rock was sold several times to help bail individual heirs out of debt.

It was acquired in 1911 by Mrs. Evalyn McClean, who had the diamond set to her own preferences. She flamboyantly wore it as a pendant on a diamond necklace until her death. In 1949, after McClean's death, Harry Winston Inc. purchased the Hope diamond from McClean's estate, along with her entire jewelry collection. The Hope diamond was donated to the Smithsonian in 1958. It draws people from all over the world who view this 45.52 carat gem with its beautiful blue hues. Its exquisite shape and setting is surrounded by sixteen white diamonds.

Along with the Hope Diamond, the Natural History Museum showcases a myriad of rare jewels and expensive jewelry from all around the world. These collections were once owned by kings, queens, dynasties, and prestigious families. One could spend hours walking through the displays, being filled with awe and wonder at the beauty and quality of these stones. The question begs, "Why are humans so enthralled with gems and jewels?" What is it about their radiance and brilliance that draws us so unapologetically?

Just as our eyes are drawn to the bling of life, God created us to be drawn to Him. When we look into scripture, the descriptions of God's glory is often compared to bright and precious gems. Ezekiel describes God's throne like a sapphire, and He who sits on the throne is likened unto the brightness and brilliance of a rainbow (see Ezekiel 1:26-28). John describes the One seated on the throne as having the appearance of jasper and carnelian, and around the throne it was like a rainbow with the resemblance of an emerald (see Revelation 4:3)

Our culture has created a view of Heaven as a place of fluffy clouds where angels flit from one mass of condensed water vapor to the next, playing their harps and being ethereal. Instead, Heaven is described as a place that is so radiant that we are primed to revel in God's presence and in awe of His holiness. Consider the jewels mentioned in the description of the holy city in Revelation 21: "The wall was made of jasper, and the city of pure gold, as pure as glass. The foundations of the city walls were decorated with every kind of precious stone. The first foundation was jasper, the second sapphire, the third chalcedony [agate], the fourth emerald, the fifth sardonyx, the sixth carnelian [ruby], the seventh chrysolite, the eighth beryl, the ninth topaz, the tenth chrysoprase [turquoise], the eleventh jacinth, and the twelfth amethyst" (Revelation 21:18-21). Now THAT is a jewelry collection!

This description of Heaven is grounded in hope! This future city for the beloved of God is solid and sure. It is beautiful and sparkling, without any need for light. The fact that the walls and streets are made with precious metals and stones points to the fact that our worship and gratefulness to God is more priceless than any earthly treasure. Our hope points forward to a future of no more tears, pain, or sorrow. However, the Rock of Hope is available in the here and now as well. The hope of Christ is what we want to pass on to our families, more than any earthly possessions.

During a Sunday morning service in June, our congregation was celebrating graduations. Students from junior high, high school, and college, lined up in front of the church. The youth pastor spoke words of encouragement and hope to them and we all prayed over these young people. A verse was placed on the screens in front as a reminder of what they should continue to build their lives on as they begin the next chapter. "He will be the sure foundation for your times, a rich store of salvation and wisdom and knowledge; the fear of the Lord is the key to this treasure" (Isaiah 33:6).

One of the high school seniors in this group of graduates was Ben Schaefer. His family willingly shared their story of God's foundation in their lives. Mark Schaefer, Alaskan Airline pilot and patriarch of this group, grew up in a home where church was important—it was their life. It was never a question for him whether he believed in God. It's just the way it was. Mark went through the whole Lutheran program, had his first communion, became an altar assistant, and went through confirmation. He was immersed in the ways of the church, the creeds, and the prayers.

Mark recognizes now that it wasn't about a personal relationship with Jesus at that time. It was more about leaning on the faith he had been taught as he grew up.

Mark started to attend Olive Knolls Church in college with some former high school friends, but he wasn't really connected. He went on Sundays, more out of obligation and habit than anything else. The rest of the week, and especially the weekends, Mark admits to hanging around with people who were going in a different direction from the one he had been taught to pursue. One Sunday morning, after a particularly late and rowdy Saturday night, he turned off his alarm and decided he didn't need church. The next week, in his words, "was horrific...no peace, no joy, no comfort, no nothing! Just turmoil." By Wednesday he couldn't take it. He got down on his knees and prayed. He let God know he needed Him, he needed help, and he needed people around him to help him through this process.

Within twenty-four hours he received a call from an acquaintance at Olive Knolls wanting to know if he would be willing to join their worship band. They needed a guitar player, and Mark fit the bill. It was the beginning of the answer to his prayer! It helped him stay connected to a church body, engaged in service, and grounded with solid friends. In addition, Mark joined Intervarsity Christian Fellowship at the University the fall of his sophomore year. Through Intervarsity's meetings and Bible studies, he met Julia.

Julia is a sixth grade teacher. Her background was quite different from Mark's. She grew up in a family who seldom, if ever, darkened the church doors. In her senior year of high school, she was invited by a friend to a youth event. It was at that time, at Nipomo Baptist Church, that she said the sinner's prayer and was baptized. Julia recalled that it was important to her to move as far away from home as she could possibly afford to go to college. She applied and was accepted to Cal State University of Bakersfield (CSUB). She remembers sitting by herself one day feeling very lonely. Someone from Intervarsity Christian Fellowship noticed her and invited her to their lunch meeting. She figured she might as well. She knew no one here, and this might provide an opportunity to make some connections.

Through Intervarsity and an invitation to Olive Knolls, Julia gained some important mentors in her life. Her first Bible study with Intervarsity examined the New Testament book of Second Timothy. It dawned on her how intimate and personal God's letter was to her. The Bible study leaders from the campus club are still people Mark and Julia are in contact with to this day, as prayer partners and friends who can offer sound advice and fellowship. At Olive Knolls, Julia met Robert and Kelly Savage. They had a huge impact on her as well. Kelly, especially, showed Julia what it looked like to be a tender, loving mom. She showed grace and shared her faith so naturally. That's when Julia had a rededication to Christ. She recognized that there was so much more beyond baptism. Jesus desired a relationship with her.

It is strikingly obvious how personal invitations can impact someone's life in ways we'll never know. We often let our fears or our insecurities keep us from asking someone to church, to a church-sponsored event, to lunch, or to coffee. Maybe it's time to get over ourselves and listen to God's promptings. Here is evidence of two amazing lives that were changed because of invitations to church, to a Bible study, and to a campus club. As we love God and love people, that love will cast out fear. "For God did not give us a spirit of timidity, but a spirit of power, of love and of self-discipline" (2 Timothy 1:7).

Mark and Julia eventually got married and began a family. They had three amazing children. Ben, their oldest, is heading to Northwest Nazarene University in the fall of 2019. His faith journey was a result of parents who began to see the importance of being purposeful in teaching their own kids about God. Having seen the impact of mentors on their own lives, they determined to help bring mentors (besides themselves) into the lives of their children as well. Ben took drum lessons from a gentleman named Scott Rhodes. At the beginning of each new school year, Scott would take Ben to lunch. He would have Ben sign or renew a contract in which he agreed to practice his drum lessons. Also included in the contract was that Ben would read the Bible each week and be willing to discuss it with Scott after each lesson.

Because of his parents and people like Mr. Rhodes, Ben was walking on **solid ground** early in his life. During his freshman year of high school, one of his class assignments was to begin to discover strengths and weaknesses that might point to a potential career. As Ben was walking to school one day, he took it a step further and asked God what he wanted for him. He said he sensed as clear as day that he was being called into youth ministry. He saw God's hand in the next few years as he played drums on the church worship team, as he went on mission trips with the youth group, and as he continued to seek God's will for his life. His life verse has become, "Have I not commanded you? Be strong and courageous. Do not be terrified; do not be discouraged, for the Lord your God will be with you wherever you go" (Joshua 1:9). Ben said that he knows that no matter what comes his way, God will be with him.

Addie, the Schaefer's daughter, will soon be a high school junior. She plays volleyball and basketball for Bakersfield Christian High School (BCHS). For her, switching to a Christian high school has really helped her grow in her faith. As a very timid child, clinging to her mom, she shared how the children's pastor, Pastor Debbie Hanson, helped pull her out of her shell. Debbie invited Addie to be on the kids' worship team, shared God's Word in a natural and real way, and encouraged her to live a life with Jesus. Now at BCHS, Addie enjoys studying the Bible each day, attending chapel once a week, and sharing with teachers who openly speak about their walk with Jesus. Her Spanish teacher is an especially close mentor who has helped her open up in conversations about God. She continues to be challenged to be in the Word daily and her relationship with God is getting stronger.

Jack, their youngest, was playing in a basketball tournament at Family Camp while the rest of the family was taking a quick break from the action to share their stories. Jack is also growing up learning about God. He is already serving and mentoring boys younger than himself. He recently was a co-counselor at kids' camp. He poured himself into the boys in his cabin, accepting and loving on them throughout the week. His example during worship, as he sang and had fun with the motions and upbeat songs, was particularly noticed by one of these young vulnerable kids who shared in a Sunday service highlighting the youth. He said, "I never knew worshiping Jesus could be so fun, but Jack showed me."

Mark and Julia recognize and are examples of living out the commandments of God. They don't just talk the talk, they walk the walk. They know that God has helped them through this life as they have attempted to serve Him in their careers, raise their family, and show others of His goodness. It's God, not a valuable diamond, who brings us hope for our descendants and their futures! Though the Hope diamond was named after its owner, Henry Philip Hope, Our God, the Rock of Hope, is named for His character and consistency. God draws us to Himself, just as we are drawn to the beauty of earthly treasures. The Shaefers have found that God, Our Rock and Hope, is the key to true and lasting treasure.

Soil-Sifting Summary

- We are created to be drawn to God and His glory just as we are drawn to radiant jewels.
- Heaven is described as a beautiful place for us to eternally worship God.
- It is strikingly obvious how personal invitations can impact someone's life in ways we'll never know. We often let our fears or our insecurities get in the way. Maybe it's time to get over ourselves and listen to God's promptings.
- Like Ben, we can be assured that no matter what comes our way, whether we are 9 or 99, God will be with us.
- Don't just talk the talk, walk the walk.
- God helps us through this life as we attempt to serve Him in our careers, raise families, and show others of His goodness. He brings us hope for our descendants and their future!!!
- The key to the true treasure, God our Rock and Hope, is trusting and serving the Lord.

Digging into God's Word

- Ezekiel 1:26-28
- Revelation 4:3
- Revelation 21:18-21
- 1 John 4:18; 2 Timothy 1:7
- Joshua 1:9
- Deuteronomy 6:4-9
- Jeremiah 31:17; Isaiah 33:6

Extracting Truths and Treasures

Chapter 26

RENOVATION

"See, I am doing a new thing! Now it springs up; do you not perceive it? I am making a way in the desert and streams in the wasteland." Isaiah 43:19

The popularity of home improvement shows has skyrocketed in the past decade or two. The Home and Garden Television (HGTV) channel began in 1994. They steadily increased the number of shows, especially those that focused on flipping houses. ABC's *Extreme Makeover: Home Edition* aired from 2003-2012. Within the first year it was rated in the top 20 television shows.

It is certainly entertaining to watch homes being transformed in an hour. You can get caught up in the demolition, cheer on the latest and greatest installments of floors and walls, and keep abreast of the latest trends in home decorating—all from the comfort of your recliner in your own home.

As we were getting to remodel our twenty-seven-year-old home, our ten-year-old granddaughter, a great fan of HGTV, was excited to do a walkthrough to give us her home improvement ideas. She made her way through each room, telling us which walls she would take down, paint colors she would use, and flooring she thought would look great. She seemed genuinely disappointed when we told her we were painting over a trailing vine that had been painted in our front entry way. From lighting ideas to closet adjustments, she was definitely on her game!

The idea of having everything once again look new and fresh is exciting. However, in reality, nothing is more disruptive to your life than a house renovation. The **solid ground** you call your home is suddenly upside down and sideways. We experienced this first hand when we decided to give our house a make-over. It started slowly. We began to unpack cupboards, setting aside all the unnecessary STUFF we had somehow collected along the way. There were three piles: store, toss, or sell. The carpet came up, leaving cement floors. The pictures came down, leaving our walls bare and sad. The furniture was removed and stacked in our garage. The date was set for our yard sale.

Even before the serious demolition had begun, there was dust everywhere. Bidders began to stream in as we tried to get the lowest price for the best quality of work. The projects began to grow as we realized that if we changed the counters, we would need to get new sinks. New sinks needed updated fixtures. Change in paint color meant new flooring. New flooring demanded fresh baseboards. Fresh baseboards made the window trim look old and tired. Every decision begat another decision.

To be honest, I'm not a great decision maker. Walking into a tile store overwhelmed me immediately. The number of light fixtures in the lighting store was mind-boggling. Who knew there were so many shades of white paint? Flooring not only came in a variety of colors and shapes, but we also had to decide on the type of material. The small samples we were able to bring home were not large enough to see the big picture. My natural reaction was either to withdraw or get frustrated and shut down. My husband was a very patient man during this time. He quickly realized that the best time to shop was in the morning hours when we were both fresh and ready to go. At the end of each day we made ourselves stop and regroup for the next day. It was a work in progress, for sure.

One of the things we knew we needed to do was to keep our eye on the prize, the end result. As difficult as it could be along the way, the final product was going to be beautiful and inviting. Eventually, the decisions would be final, the sub-contractors chosen, and the coordination of the décor complete. We were looking forward to that day, but in the meantime we would endure our trial with joy (most of the time).

There are so many parallels between home remodels and our walk with Christ. Upon receiving Christ into your heart and life, He takes the old and makes it new! He removes our sin—and the brokenness it has produced—and exchanges it for His peace, hope, joy, and righteousness. We experience a new spring in our step, a renewed smile on our face, and an exciting fresh purpose for our life. These changes bubble from deep within as the burden of bearing our own shame is lifted.

But God is not through with us yet! He promises that "...He who began a good work in you will carry it on to completion until the day of Christ Jesus" (Philippians 1:6). This means that we will need renovations and remodeling throughout our lives. When God begins His work in us, He might start by changing out the flooring. He establishes our lives on a solid rock instead of the shifting sand we stood on previously. When the flooring is in place, it makes our paint look dingy. As His word sheds light on the marks and nicks and cracks in our pasts, He reveals Himself and wants to refurbish those blemishes with His love and grace. He wants us to feel whole and fresh.

Now that our floors and walls are under God's wonderful care, He begins to ask for permission to move from room to room. He never forces His way in, but waits patiently, offering to take our burdens and give us His yoke, which is easy, and His burden, which is light (see Matthew 11:30). For some reason, we tend to resist. We are "comfortable" with the way things are. We don't want to go through the temporary inconvenience of change. We think that if we have been this way this long, why change now?

But God always has our best in mind. "No discipline seems pleasant at the time, but painful. **Later on**, however, it produces a harvest of righteousness and peace for those who have been trained by it (Hebrews 12:11)." (Emphasis is mine.) We can't get caught up in the answers we don't see in the present, but we can know that God is working on, in, and through us to make us more like Himself. I have come to think of our faith during times of trials, difficulties, or discipline as "later-on faith." When the "later-on" comes, we can look back and see how His hand was moving all along.

This type of faith is also our opportunity to say "Yes," to Jesus. "Yes" to getting rid of an old habit, and "Yes" to replacing it with the fruit of joy or patience or kindness. "Yes" to routing our worry and anxiety, and "Yes" to a life of peace and self-control. "Yes" to tearing out our judgmental spirit, and "Yes" to a spirit of grace and love.

I met a man named Joe who came by my book table at an event the other day. Joe and I began to share about the story God is writing in his life. Joe had been in prison, angry and hurt, shaking his fist at God. God listened to Joe, even in his anger. He began to work on the restoration of his life in miraculous ways. Eventually

Joe's fourteen-year sentence was reduced to three years. When he was released he began a prison ministry. Today he is on fire for God, is the spiritual leader in his home, and continues his ministry through his local church. God had to take the prison bars off of his heart and soul before he could begin to see God's potential in his life.

It would be ludicrous to think of Joe begging to go back to serve more time in prison. He is finished with the old life and moving victoriously forward. It would be like going to the dump and picking through the rubble to find our old broken counter tile or demolished flooring. Unfortunately, we sometimes do this. We go for a few months allowing the renovation to begin, but before it is completed, we head to the dump to pick up the broken pieces. We futilely try to put the pieces back together.

Fortunately, God is patient, redemptive, and forgiving. When we are done with our futile attempt to build up our own lives, putting unsightly patches over the things we struggle with, God comes in and does "a new thing." He transforms our pain into purpose. He creates beauty from the mess. He makes "a way in the desert and rivers in the wasteland." The question is, "Do you not perceive it?" He is ready to reveal it to us. Let Him bring on the renovation!

Soil-Sifting Summary

- Upon receiving Christ into your heart and life, He takes the old and makes it new! He removes our sin—and the brokenness that it has produced—and exchanges it for His peace, hope, joy, and righteousness.
- God is not finished with us!
- He never forces His way in, but waits patiently, offering to take our burdens and give us His yoke, which is easy, and His burden. which is light.
- We can face our times of trials, difficulties, or discipline with "later-on faith." When the "later-on" comes, we can look back and see how His hand was moving all along.
- When we are done with our futile attempt to build up our own lives, putting unsightly patches over the things we struggle with, God comes in and does "a new thing." He transforms our pain into purpose. He creates beauty from the mess.

Digging into God's Word

- 2 Corinthians 5:17
- Philippians 1:6
- Matthew 11:28-30
- Hebrews 12:11
- Revelation 21:5
- Isaiah 43:19

Extracting Truths and Treasures

Chapter 27

UPROOTED

So then, just as you received Christ Jesus as Lord, continue to
live in him, rooted and built up in him, strengthened in the faith as
you were taught, and overflowing with thankfulness.
Colossians 2:6-7

Seventy-six year-old Emily White grew up in a little
town called Monument, New Mexico, so she came by her
Southern drawl naturally. It was evident as we began our
conversation that she had a joy for life. A couple of her passions,
gardening and cooking, helped shape her life's trajectory. God had
placed these passions in her, and He had amazing ways He planned
to fulfill the desires of her heart.

As she began to talk about the different places they had lived, I
actually became a bit confused as I tried to keep up with all of the
moves she and Leon had made throughout their lives. Emily found
purpose and connection in each of the places they lived, but she
never quite felt completely rooted. There was always a sense that
God was preparing her for something more.

One of the places that always felt like home was the Nazarene
campground in New Mexico. Bonita Park was the place they went
for family camp, kids' camps, retreats and conferences. Emily said
that each time they drove up to the camp she felt like a snake who
was shedding its skin. Since a snake's skin doesn't grow with the
snake, snakes shed their old skin to allow for further growth. As
they shed off the old skin, they leave behind the parasites that have

attached to it. Participating in the services and activities at the Bonita Park campground meant a time of growth for Emily. It was always a place where she felt she could shed the things that were sucking life from her and move forward in her walk with God.

At one point they settled in a small town called Ruidoso, New Mexico, not far from Bonita Park. Emily was working for State Farm Insurance Company at the time. There was a restaurant that she passed each day on her way to work called the Red Rooster. It had closed down and was sitting empty. God was pulling her toward this property. Finally she confided in Leon that she had always wanted to start a restaurant of her own. Leon laughed at her, but she convinced him to at least stop and check it out. The owners were anxious to rent it, but it was really a dive. It only seated seventeen people on the inside and was in need of a lot of elbow grease and some updating. They made a deal to pay six hundred dollars a month to rent it.

With Emily still working at State Farm, they prepared the restaurant, called *Southern Accent*, for their first day of business. What an appropriate name! Signs in front of the restaurant advertised opening day as the day after Thanksgiving in 1995. To their amazement, on that day the parking lot was completely full and there was a line of people waiting to be served. Emily had never even worked in a restaurant, so she had no idea what to do. Their son caught on fast. He was their grill cook, and he kept the line moving. Over time, he got to know the customers by name, and knew what they usually ordered. He was a real asset to the business.

Emily eventually quit her job at State Farm because of the growth of the restaurant. They moved tables onto a newly built deck which increased the serving capacity to about thirty-five people. It still wasn't enough, so they hired someone to clear out and level areas under the surrounding pine trees. With tables under the trees, they increased seating to about one hundred twenty-five people. They had many returning customers, many of whom would come every single day for the meals Emily cooked. She would decide on her menu, which was seldom the same from week to week, and she would send out the choice of fare for the next day in a fax to about sixty phone numbers each evening.

It was a mission field as well as a business. They played Christian music (often Revised Standard Version CD's). They prayed with people and looked for those who seemed down and out. One day Leon talked to a lady whose countenance was especially sad. A couple of days later the lady's sister came back in and thanked him for taking an interest. It had made a difference!

Emily also used her business to cater for companies and private parties. She would cater brunch for State Farm conferences at the convention center. She catered dinner for the Indian school on the outskirts of town for about three hundred students. She got lost one time trying to find a chuck wagon out in the middle of nowhere for a rancher's surprise birthday party. There was no lack of business. During this time God was teaching and training and preparing Emily for her future. She was getting valuable experience preparing for and serving large groups.

After three years at this location, the building sold and she had to move the restaurant to a new location. It was not as convenient a spot for customers, and it didn't go as well. It lacked the ambiance and feel of the other place. It wasn't as visible, and there was limited parking. Two years later, they moved the restaurant to

Capitan for two more years before selling the business. Even after seven years of cooking, Emily said she really wasn't ready to give up serving food, so she began to volunteer in the Bonita Park camp kitchen. They were definitely impressed with her work, and she was hired as director of food services. She was in charge of the kitchen as well as the campground's restaurant called Broken Bread.

Their next move was to Wichita, Kansas. She continued to use her talents as she catered for church dinners, including a barbeque brisket dinner for about six hundred people. She described it as really fun. You know you are in your wheelhouse when serving that many people is "fun." Their uprooting continued as they made their way to Bakersfield for a brief period of time. During that stay, they attended Olive Knolls Nazarene Church. After a short while, they decided to move to Oklahoma to help with Leon's brother and sister-in-law who were getting up in years. They became good friends with their neighbors and lived close to one of their daughters, but after four years they were feeling that it might be time to move back to Bakersfield.

They put their house on the market, but it received no action. Maybe they weren't supposed to move after all, or maybe they needed to wait on God's timing. After taking the house off the market, one day out of the blue their real estate agent called and said there was a lady who was interested in seeing their house. They told her the house wasn't for sale, but agreed to show it. The house was bought with cash that afternoon, and a contract with a thirty-day escrow was signed.

Leon didn't want to move their furniture again, especially since they were planning to down-size. They decided to have an estate sale to get rid of everything. Before the sale, Emily wrote an amount on a piece of paper that she felt they needed to get from their transactions. When all was said and done, they only had one small table left. When Emily added up the money, they had made $68 more than what she had written down as their goal total. It seemed that God was uprooting them again and orchestrating this move.

Once back in Bakersfield, Emily and Leon returned to Olive Knolls Church. For months Emily would sit in church and wonder why they were here. What was God's purpose for her? Then one Sunday she heard someone sharing about the Celebrate Recovery (CR) ministry and feeding the Friday night participants. After prayer meeting one night, Emily asked Pastor Darren Reed, if they needed any help in CR. She felt she could prepare meals for them for less than two dollars per person. Pastor Darren's eyebrows raised, and he said, "Really?" He connected her with the CR pastoral staff, and after a couple of weeks of helping out, Emily was given free reign.

People seem to enjoy the food. Emily is in her sweet spot. It is her ministry. She said that she may not be able to talk to people on the street, but she can prepare a meal and make people happy. She prepares food for one hundred or more people each week, planning the menu, shopping for the food, and cooking. The new music minister, Justin, told her he hadn't seen the same thing on the menu twice in the nine months he had been there. She truly receives joy in serving people in this way!

It doesn't stop with just the cooking. Emily makes a point to learn everyone's name. She seeks out the new people and tries to make them feel welcome. She enjoys watching people change from week to week. Their countenance literally changes as they begin to let people and Jesus into their lives. She now receives hugs and words of affirmation from those she is getting to know.

Emily keeps in communication through text and Facebook with many of the people she is becoming acquainted with. She says it's easy to love them because she recognizes that person could have been her! She had watched first hand as her husband struggled with alcoholism through their earlier years. Because of her experiences, she understands that the struggles they face affect their families and loved ones. She realizes that they need help to conquer the disease of addiction that they face. They need love! Her heart is overflowing.

As we talked, I was getting the bigger picture. Now it was making a little more sense why they moved around so much. Leon's alcoholism caused him to be restless. He was running from God and from decisions and hurt and pain. In each uprooting, God had a specific part of His plan He was setting into motion. He was bringing them to a place of **solid ground** where they could establish some deeper roots. Leon is free of his addiction and joins her as much as possible in the ministry. I think they are here for the long haul!

God was grooming Emily back when she opened the restaurant. He knew where she was going to be in 2019. She gained knowledge a little at a time, and through much trial and error. Right now she is in the place where God wants her. She has a mission to fulfill each week, and it is giving her a new sense of purpose. It doesn't matter what age or stage we are in, God never stops using us for His glory if we are open to His leading!

We ended our visit with a tour of Emily's garden. They have a small apartment with a little outside patio. This twelve by eight feet space is outfitted with several levels of shelving on which potted plants have been placed. She is growing tomatoes, green beans, red bell peppers, okra, radishes, spinach and cucumbers. I was given a kumquat from her tree and had to be reminded how to eat it. Just as Emily is allowing these plants to reach their roots deep into the rich soil in order to grow delicious vegetables and fruit, God has allowed Emily to be rooted and built up in Him. She is bearing the fruit of her labor and is overflowing with thankfulness.

Soil-Sifting Summary

- God is always preparing and equipping us for His future purpose.
- In order to grow we have to leave the old behind so we can move forward with God.
- Wherever God plants us becomes our mission field.
- We must wait and trust in God's timing.
- God uses our experiences and location to establish our roots in Him.

Digging into God's Word

- Hebrews 13:20-21
- Ephesians 4:22-24
- Acts 1:8
- Psalm 27:14
- Colossians 2:6-7

Extracting Truths and Treasures

Chapter 28

VALLEY FEVER

Praise the Lord, O my soul; all my inmost being, praise his holy name. Praise the Lord, O my soul, and forget not all his benefits— who...heals all your diseases.

Psalm 103:1-3

Those who have lived in the Central Valley in California for very long know about Valley Fever. It is a fungal infection caused by Coccidioides, organisms found in the soil in specific regions. Bakersfield is one of those regions. As farming, construction, or wind disrupts the soil, the spores can be stirred into the air. Breathing the fungi into your lungs can cause anywhere from mild to severe symptoms that mimic the flu. This can make it hard to diagnose quickly, as patients are treated for their fever, cough, chills, headache, fatigue, and joint aches. As time progresses and the typical treatments don't appear to be effective, a special blood test can detect the disease. It is treated with an antifungal medication, but it can take months to fully recover.

In October of 2012, when the prescribed antibiotics weren't improving my "pneumonia," I was eventually diagnosed with Valley Fever. I ended up taking about two and a half months off of work. I can remember getting up, taking a shower, and having to go back to bed because I didn't have enough energy to blow dry my hair. My appetite was low and I lost a lot of weight. (Oh, why didn't that last?) This was my first experience with anything that severe. I received such great support from my church friends who visited me in the hospital and brought meals to our house when I got home. My husband and other family were amazing, supporting me in prayer and taking up the extra chores. The people at work were extremely understanding and gracious. Many people had to take on extra responsibilities and workload to get through those months.

God was especially close during this trial. I had to depend on Him. I had to depend on others, which was foreign to my lifestyle. God was my strength when I had little or none. I let praise music flow through my spirit, and allowed myself to rest. I learned to listen to my body as I began to recover so that I didn't overdo it. God clearly carried me through this desert experience. Though the spores in the earth's dust had caused suffering, God's **solid ground** sustained me through it. After 6 months I got the clearance from my infectious disease specialist. I was completely healed from Valley Fever. Praise the Lord! At some point I wrote this humorous account of my hospital experience.

It was 3 days before Halloween when I was ordered to go to an Emergency Room to get checked into the hospital. I ended up being diagnosed with Valley Fever. The signs and symptoms in some blood work were very concerning for the doctor, and he called me at home that Sunday afternoon to take action quickly. Quick is a relative term when it comes to ER. We were there for about 11 hours before I was finally admitted to a hospital bed around midnight. The experience was grueling, but rather than be upset and bitter, I decided to find some humor in it and make some comparisons to the upcoming holiday.

First of all there were the spooky sounds. The myriads of people in the waiting room and holding areas had come for a variety of reasons. Some were moaning in pain. Babies and a crazy African American woman were screaming and crying. I finally had to leave an area I had been encamped in for over four hours because if I heard one more person retching, I was going to lose my mind (much less my own lunch). I know it's an ER, but have some decency to put those people in a sound-proof room!

Then there were beings wanting my blood. They were not vampires, of course, but phlebotomists. Drawing blood is their job, and some are better at it than others. My blood was drawn twice that night as well as several times during my hospital stay. In the hospital room, they would usually arrive at 6:00 in the morning, when I was still sound asleep. They would slowly open the squeaky door, turn on the light and waltz in announcing that they were here for a blood draw. I have a sneaking suspicion that the reason they do it this way is so that you will not be awake enough to be able to focus on them and recognize them later in public.

Next came the mysterious disappearing object—which happened to be my medical chart! After waiting for several hours in what they call a wrap-around room, everyone had wrapped around except me! They typically don't allow family members to be in there with you because they need all the chairs for the constant rotation of people who are needing a breathing treatment or an IV drip of some kind. I finally called my husband back and asked him to inquire at the desk as to the status of my situation. Funny, they couldn't find my chart. He persisted, the person in charge kept looking, and finally located me (or at least my medical records) in the back of a long stack of clipboards with other charts waiting for results from the aforementioned blood draw results. Refusing to take no for an answer, my husband inquired as to why my results were taking so long. The trusty computer showed that the results had indeed been in for a couple of hours, but had somehow been overlooked. My chart was immediately moved to the front.

The second occurrence of the missing chart was when it was drawing close to midnight. The doctor had assured me around 10:00 PM that there was a room and a bed upstairs being prepared for me and that I would be transported soon. My weary husband left at that time feeling assured that I would be taken care of soon. I was now the lone soul in the wrap-around room. I took the best recliner that the room had to offer and continued waiting. The minutes drained the clock. When the next person they brought to join me was another individual who was retching her guts, I had had it! I walked out and explained that even though this was an ER, I could not take another round of listening to someone throw up, and where was my room! The person on duty began to scramble and surprisingly could not come up with my chart!

She checked the computer and clearly found that there was a room ready for me. However, she was hesitant to send me upstairs without my chart. She frantically looked hither and yon before finally giving the order to have me delivered to my accommodations and that the chart would have to follow when found. Talk about a Halloween scare! As I arrived, a friendly admitting nurse stood over me saying, I've been looking for you. Your chart has been up here for a while and I kept calling down to the lobby for you. The LOBBY? Why would I have been in the lobby? Just give me a bed and some pain meds—my head is killing me!

The third incident of my missing chart occurred the next morning. I was transported by gurney downstairs to have an ultrasound done of my liver, which seemed to be the cause of all of this hullabaloo in the first place. After being gelled up and caressed with the wand for about twenty minutes, the specialist realized her machine wasn't working. Ten minutes later we were at it again, this time successfully. My transporter came back to get me and coincidentally was the same lady who had brought me down. We chatted a bit, got on the elevator, and got off...on the wrong floor. I asked her where she was taking me and very coherently was able to give her my room number. She looked at the chart on the bed and asked if I was Mrs. So-and-So. When I shook my head no, she sighed and said she thought that this was the wrong room because she remembered picking me up (thank God). Who knows where I would have ended up and what surgery would have been performed unnecessarily on me. I guess the chart had once again mysteriously disappeared, but it evidently got sorted out because the doctor had the results of the ultrasound that afternoon (at least I hope they were mine).

Added to these events were blobs of unidentifiable matter brought to me on a tray faithfully at 8:00 AM, 12:00 Noon, and 6:00 PM each day. I believe it was supposed to be food, but I use that term lightly. At least for day two I was able to place my order ahead of time and I strategically circled all of the things that were as close to their true form as possible—milk, yogurt, fresh fruit. With a little, ok a lot of salt, you could kind of get a taste out of some of it, whatever it was.

One morning, as I was finishing up some Special K (how can you mess that up), I glanced out my door that was open to the hall. There was a gentleman walking down the hall. He was sixty-ish with a gray scruffy beard, pale face, and yes black socks. The reason I know the color of his socks so well is because I was trying not to look up. He was arrayed in his hospital gown, pushing his IV cart in front of him, trying to get some exercise in the hall. I'm glad he was coming toward me because I did not want to see what was on the open side of that lovely gown. I began to chuckle. His halting steps (good for him for getting his exercise) with his arms out in front of him pushing his IV cart reminded me of those horror flicks where the walking dead are roaming about the cemetery. Later that day I joined the ranks as I took my laps around the wing.

My walk was also a good excuse to get away from my room and the noisy family that was visiting my roommate. They finally left the afternoon after her surgery, and I enjoyed some peace and quiet. Peace that was very short-lived. "I'm here to take your vitals"...AGAIN. Every four hours my caregiver would come to put a vice around my arm, allegedly to take my blood pressure. She would take my temperature, ask about all my toilet habits of the day, encourage me to drink plenty of water, and happily skip about her business. Whether in the middle of a nap or the middle of

246

the night, rain or shine, sleet or hail, the caregiver would never fail!

Though it may not be apparent, I really was well taken care of. The nursing staff through each shift change was friendly, helpful and truly concerned about their patients. There is something to be said about being able to lay in bed and push a button any time you need something. On the day I was released, Halloween Day, one of my caregivers came dressed in a Halloween costume. It was a reminder that life was still going on out there, and there was hope for my situation.

Disease and hospitalization are really no laughing matter. I am grateful that there was a cure for my situation. There is also a cure for the Valley of the Shadow of Death. We do not have to fear for God is with us through our trials. He gets to the root cause of our spiritual infirmities and heals our diseases.

Soil-Sifting Summary

- God is especially close during our trials.
- We put total dependence on God when we have no strength within ourselves.
- God carries us through our desert experiences.
- There is also a cure for the Valley of the Shadow of Death. We do not have to fear for God is with us through our trials.
- God uses the great care of doctors and nurses to bring about our return to health, but praise is due to the One who heals our diseases.

Digging into God's Word

- Deuteronomy 31:8
- 2 Corinthians 1:9
- Deuteronomy 1:29–31
- Psalm 23:4
- Psalm 103

Extracting Truths and Treasures

Chapter 29

NOT A HAIR ON YOUR

HEAD

But not a hair of your head will perish. By standing firm you will gain life. Luke 21:18-19

On September 3, 2017, UCLA's football team made a historic come back against Texas A & M. They were down 10 to 44 well into the 3rd quarter. With under nine minutes left in the game Josh Rosen threw five unanswered touchdowns to bring his Bruins to a 45-44 victory. I remember the day because we were at the game! The elated Texas fans were quickly deflated as they watched their team's lead slowly fade away. We had talked to a few of those fans before the game began.

Welcoming them to California, we asked them if they had been effected by the recent flooding around Southeastern Texas. About a week earlier Hurricane Harvey had increased from a slow-moving tropical storm in the Gulf of Mexico to a Category four hurricane that made landfall on August 25, 2017. Though the one hundred thirty mile per hour winds began to die down, the storm stalled over Houston and much of southeast Texas. During that time, the storm dumped a year's worth of rain in less than a week. On August 29, 2017, two flood control reservoirs had breached, increasing water levels throughout Houston.

The Texas A & M fans had not personally been effected, but they had many friends and acquaintances in the state whose lives had been changed forever. Records indicated that 13,000,000 people had been affected, 135,000 homes had been damaged or destroyed, one million cars were wrecked, and the death toll was eighty-eight people. As we shared in the grief over this catastrophe, they in turn empathized with us over the fires the state of California was facing. As they had flown into LAX they said it appeared as if the entire state was ablaze.

California was in the latter two years of a seven year drought. What they were seeing from the air was probably up to thirteen partially contained wildfires throughout several counties. This was only a fraction of the many fires that occurred throughout 2017 and 2018. It seemed rather ironic that the over-abundance of water that Texas had experienced was so elusive in California. We were, in that moment, not sports rivals but friends who had an instant deep connection over the pain and suffering of our neighbors and friends.

Before California's three-hundred seventy-six weeks of drought ended, we would see many more wildfires. Some were caused by nature's course, others were started because of man's carelessness, evil intent, or negligence. One of the most devastating fires occurred on November 8, 2018, in Paradise, California. The fire was sparked by electrical transmission lines owned and operated by Pacific Gas & Electric. It spread quickly due to the heavy grass cover that had grown after a wet spring. Followed by the hot summer months and an unusually dry fall, the grass was perfect fuel for an explosive blaze. The flames were fanned on the day of the fire by continual, hot, dry, gusting winds. It is estimated that the communities of Concow and Paradise were destroyed within the first six hours of the inferno starting. Ninety-five percent of the structures were lost. The death toll was eighty-six lives.

Teresa Reid, the client service director for Paradise's Pregnancy Center, remembered the night before the fire. She was helping plan and prepare for the center's fundraising banquet that was to occur the next evening. She remembered thinking that she hoped the high winds wouldn't create any electrical blackouts that might affect their event. Exhausted from all the preparations, Teresa fell into bed, only to be awakened at four in the morning by the gusting winds. She got up, took an herbal sleep aid, moved her phone into the bathroom, and went back to sleep.

Teresa is convinced God woke her up that morning about eight. She was feeling pretty groggy as she made her way to the bathroom, where she saw that she had missed multiple phone calls. She called back her daughter first, since she was supposed to babysit her grandkids later that day. Her daughter's first words were, "Have you evacuated?" Now being wide awake, she called her husband, Chris. He expressed his concern as well, explaining that the fire was really ramping up, and he told her she needed to get out fast! She sensed the urgency in her husband's normally calm demeanor. He let her know that he would be staying at the school where he was principal and superintendent to help fight the fire and make sure all the students and staff got to safety.

Teresa knew that God had been preparing her for this very moment. One of her adult daughters had been to the house a few weeks before. For some reason, she had gone through the house, identifying things that were precious and important to the family. Her nostalgic trip down memory lane had been like a dress rehearsal for this moment. It helped Teresa focus on grabbing a few important treasures as she was getting ready to head down the hill. God had used her daughter to help prepare the way before her.

Some of the most difficult things Teresa had to leave behind were her prayer journals, Bible and notes. One of the things that she remembered clearly journaling about in the several months previous to the fire was the sense that their world was going to be shaken. She also sensed the Holy Spirit promising her that not a hair on her head would be harmed. She had no idea that the **solid ground** of her physical home would be swept from under her, but she could rest in God's provision and protection. God would remain the foundation for her life.

There are a couple of Biblical references to the promise that "not a hair on your head will be harmed." One is in Daniel when Shadrach, Meshach and Abednego were thrown into the fiery furnace for not bowing down to the king's idol. Their trust in the one true God and their faithfulness to Him was honored through their deliverance. Their clothes and hair were not even singed by the blazing furnace that was so hot it killed the soldiers that led them to it! Glory was given to God when the king later declared that no one was to say anything against their God "for no other god can save in this way" (Daniel 3:29b).

The other reference to this promise is in Luke 21 where Jesus is talking about signs of the end of the age. He speaks of fearful events and great signs from heaven. He tells of the persecution and rejection we will face. Then He says, "But not a hair of your head will perish. By standing firm you will gain life" (Luke 21:18-19). It's not that our lives will be void of hardship. It's that by standing true and firm to God we can be assured of His faithfulness to us.

Teresa made it to Chico. She was staying in phone communication with her husband, who was still fighting the fire and taking care of others. At one point cell service was gone. The last thing Chris had said to Teresa was that he wasn't sure if he would be able to get out. If he had to, he would get in the car with their son, who was a principal at a nearby school, and just wait it out. Teresa recalls just saying over and over again in prayer, "I trust you, I trust you!" Chris and their son both made it to safety later that day. God was with them!

In the aftermath of trying to put life back in order, Teresa said they continually prayed for wisdom. There were major decisions to be made, a myriad of insurance determinations to work through, and a ton of things to replace. The trauma from the fires was an ongoing issue. Clients from the Crisis Pregnancy Center still needed counseling, and this new ordeal was adding to the suffering and pain they already had experienced. School needed to continue, and students needed to feel like there was something normal in their lives. Even though they were meeting in an unfamiliar gym with six classes together in one space, they could feel a sense of comfort being with those who had been through the same intense, life-changing crisis.

God provided the wisdom they asked for. Teresa and Chris were able to procure property within a couple months of the fire, and now have a home that is paid in full. God provided for their future retirement through this tragedy! What an unexpected blessing! Chris's school was one of the structures that endured the fire. He will be starting classes in his school building in the fall of 2019. Their perseverance through the fiery trial and seeking God's wisdom was rewarded.

Teresa has had a chance to speak about her experience to a few groups of people. One of the things she feels is important to share is how God helped her begin to deal with her own post-traumatic stress disorder (PTSD). In the months after the fire, strangely, the word "goads" kept popping into her brain. She thought it was a little weird, but the word kept coming back. She finally asked her husband if he knew anything about goads. He said it came from a Scripture verse about Paul. Teresa set out to research what God might be teaching her through this unique word.

The passage comes from Acts 26 where Paul is testifying before King Agrippa, the king of Judea from 41-44 AD. In Paul's address, he shares about how he was on the road to Damascus to persecute Christians when he was suddenly blinded by a bright light from heaven. Jesus spoke to him and said, "Saul, Saul, why do you persecute me? It is hard for you to kick against the goads" (Acts 26:14b). Kicking against the goads was a Greek proverb that referred to useless resistance. Goads were long poles or sticks with a pointed piece of iron fastened to one end. The farmer would use it to guide the oxen in the direction he needed them to go to plow the field. If they kicked against the goad, it would drive the point into their flesh, causing discomfort and pain. They would learn quickly to accept the direction of the farmer. We, who can be as stubborn as beasts, often fight against the direction that God is leading us. The consequences are never good!

What God was trying to tell Teresa was that her sleepless nights, recurring dreams, and, at times, fearful waking hours were a result of her kicking against what she had learned throughout her days of walking with her Savior. She realized that she had habits in place prior to the fire that she needed to return to, habits of resting in the Lord and counting on His strength. When she began to be still before Him and commit her days, hours, and minutes to Him, restful sleep returned. The stress and PTSD symptoms she had been having lessened each day. She was much more equipped to find personal victory and help others.

One final story from Teresa is worth telling. Still feeling anxious about certain environments, Teresa found herself dreading a trip to Target in Chico. She had to get a few items, but she was not looking forward to the crowds, the blaring piped in music, or the general noise of a public place. As she was wandering through the aisles, she saw an African American woman standing in front of a display of scissors. As Teresa drew closer, she realized that this woman was singing a Negro spiritual that was beautiful and soothing. They stood together for a few minutes before the woman spoke to her and said, "I'm sorry, I didn't realize I was singing over the music." They parted ways, but it seemed like this lady was following Teresa throughout the store, continuing to sing her beautiful lyrics. They never made eye contact, but it was as if God had sent her to Teresa to help her through what would normally have been a routine shopping trip.

Once in her car, Teresa reflected on God's goodness. Had he sent her an angel? Was she a Christian woman who was being obedient and grateful to God? Teresa wasn't sure, but she knew for certain that God was looking after her, even in the small things. Not a hair on her head had been harmed, and she was gaining life by standing firm. God was showing up and singing over her with His love, washing her with His peace and joy. Take heart! Don't hang your hands and head in despair! God takes delight in you and will quiet you with His love. He rejoices over you with singing!

Not unlike the UCLA comeback, the Paradise community is coming back. In their first high school football game since the fires stole their season the previous fall, Paradise beat their opponent soundly. It was not just about the score. The town typically shuts down for Friday night football, whether you know anyone on the team or not. The normal crowd numbers between 2000 and 2500 in this town of 27,000. For their opening season game, there were at least 5000 fans. The athletic director commented on how strong the community is and how they are becoming more and more like family. She stated that nothing will stand in their way, and they are coming back fighting. Somehow I think the angels have their own cheerleading squad that are singing and cheering the team and the town on in their come-back victory.

Soil-Sifting Summary

- God uses people and circumstances to help prepare the way before us.
- It's not that our lives will be void of hardship. It's that by standing true and firm to God we can be assured of His faithfulness to us.
- Our perseverance through trials and seeking God's wisdom will be rewarded.
- We, who can be as stubborn as beasts, often fight against the direction that God is leading us. The consequences are never good!
- When we are still before God and commit our days, hours, and minutes to Him, we find ourselves more equipped to find personal victory and help others.
- Take heart! Don't hang your hands and head in despair! God takes delight in you and will quiet you with His love. He rejoices over you with singing!

Digging into God's Word

- Malachi 3:1
- Daniel 3
- Luke 21:5-19
- James 1:2-8
- Acts 26:1-18
- Psalm 37:1-9
- Zephaniah 3:16-20

Extracting Truths and Treasures

Chapter 30
HOLY GROUND

"Do not come any closer," God said. "Take off your sandals, for the place where you are standing is holy ground." Exodus 3:5

𝓘 sat in Starbucks with Pastor Darren and his daughter, Keira. They were talking to me about their visit to The Holy Land Experience (HLE) in Orlando, Florida. It was a profound encounter for the entire family. Darren admitted that he didn't want to go at first. He wanted to go to Disney World! He was out-voted by the rest of the family, and he was at least happy that the cost wasn't going to be as great. The moment they entered the Biblical scenes, they knew they were on Holy Ground. Like the place where Moses encountered God, the **solid ground** we stand on is not holy by nature. It is made holy by the divine presence of our Holy God. His presence was real in this place!

Darren expounded a little about the gentleman who played the part of Jesus throughout the day. Darren believed the actor was created to play that part. His name is Michael Job, and he has played this role for fourteen years. His job seldom ends at the end of the workday. Even out of costume and with his hair pulled back, people recognize him all over the city in malls and restaurants, and they want a touch from "Jesus." A National Geographic article featuring HLE and the role played by Jesus, mentioned that his dad is a cop. His dad loves telling people, "Be careful, my son's Jesus!"[5]

[5] Strolich, Nina (2018, December 12). Follow the Day in the Life of a Theme Park. Retrieved from https://www.nationalgeographic.com/culture/2018/12/follow-a-day-in-life-with-theme-park-jesus-at-holy-land-usa/

Michael is from upstate New York, and has a master's degree in vocal performance. He has had roles such as Captain America at Universal Studios and Gaston in *Beauty and the Beast* at Disney World. At age twenty-eight, he found God in Times Square. His life of depression and lust turned to joy. Playing Jesus allows him to use his natural gifts, but he sees himself as an evangelist who happens to act. According to the article, and confirmed by Darren and Kiera, Michael takes time to talk and pray with people who are visiting. More often than not, the production crew is hunting him down and rushing him on stage just in time for his next performance.

As "Jesus" took time with the Reed kids, he touched and blessed each one. He prayed over them and played with them. He took an EvangeCube out of his pocket and began to share the gospel story through the use of this "toy." Kiera, who had been quietly sipping on her drink next to us, piped up, "Oh, yeah, you said we were going to get one of those!" Darren agreed that he had said that, they just hadn't made the purchase yet. Who knows but that this will become a craze among the children's ministry departments across the country! (I bet you will all be checking this out on line!)

One of the things that impressed Darren was the perspective of being Jesus to others in our world. This idea fits in perfectly with *Organic Outreach*, sharing Jesus in a natural yet purposeful way to those we connect with every day. How do we bring the gospel alive to others? You have to live it. You have to practice it. You invite people over, you get out of your comfort zone, and you become intentional about staying connected. When you **are** with people, you are tuned in to them. You speak blessings over their lives and pray for them. It's what Jesus would do! Our homes and our workplaces become holy ground because Jesus is present. People should recognize you in malls and restaurants and want a touch from "Jesus."

At the Holy Land Experience, Jesus (aka Michael Job), becomes one with the Holy Spirit. Miracles happen every day. People come to faith in the Lord. Darren surmised that this gentleman alone probably has brought more people to a relationship with Jesus than anyone else in the entire city of Orlando. Darren said watching him in action gave his wife Julie and him a new drive to not just preach the gospel, but to live it every moment! Darren gave me permission to share his Facebook post that he wrote after their day at HLE. It fills in a few more of the details and is a challenge and encouragement:

> I don't believe I have ever posted anything longer than a couple of sentences, but as I look back on the last couple of weeks in Florida with our family, I feel compelled to share some reflections which have moved my heart. For those that stick with me through this post, I pray that the Lord will stir your spirit.
>
> Orlando truly is the vacation capital of the world with more than 126 million tourists visiting in 2018. Walt Disney World Resort alone will welcome, on average, 140,000 people per day, while Universal Studios will entertain more than 30,000. Sea World will see approximately 15,000 people walk through their turnstiles, leaving countless other thrill seekers to visit the more than 100 other attractions in the Central Florida area.
>
> Tucked in the midst of options is a lesser known, even lesser attended destination called The Holy Land Experience (HLE). In short, this small operation takes visitors on a theatrical journey through the stories of the Bible as well as

offering historical artifacts and attractions that move the heart closer to God.

Our family was deeply moved by this experience as we followed the first Christians, with Peter as their guide, through their persecution and ultimate martyrdom, communicated through musical theater and multimedia beauty worthy of the Broadway stage. Along the way, Peter encouraged the fearful young church to remember the faith of their ancestors and take courage of what might come as a result of their own faith in Jesus. It takes a lot for me to be moved to tears. That said, through each station of the journey, God moved my heart in ways that has changed me in profound ways. Both Julie and I shared how this experience has somehow created a personal revival within us. To watch the compassion and power of Jesus through the stories and then identify with the uncertainties of life through Esther, David, Peter, and Mary has shaken me to the core. The icing on the cake was to watch my children touched (literally and figuratively) by Jesus' presence through the actors.

While many people will go to Fantasyland at Walt Disney World and lose themselves in the thrill of imagination which will last but a moment, we experienced the reality of God's love at work, which will last an eternity for those who say yes to Jesus. While thousands will visit Epcot and experience a possible future for humanity, we were moved to tears through the reminder of the assurance of our future hope in Jesus. While thousands may get wet by [the splash of] a large whale at Sea World, we were saturated in the presence of God through the power of His story. While many will be guided through Universal Studios to witness the magic of movies, we witnessed many people guided to say "yes" to

Jesus as their Lord and Savior for the first time. While Mickey Mouse may take a few seconds for a photo op, I watched Jesus take unsolicited time with my children...not only to take a picture, but [to] tell them the gospel story and then lay hands on each child to pray [a] blessing on them. Somehow I don't see Donald Duck offering such a prayer.

Please don't get me wrong! I love going to all the amusement parks and the memories that are generated from the experience. In fact, I'm looking forward to a time when we will visit the next theme park. However, God has reminded me what truly matters in this life and what brings true happiness. While Disney's tag line might be the Happiest Place on Earth....the life and joy that God offers through Jesus far exceeds the temporary thrill of man's attempt to satisfy through the escape of amusement. This experience at HLE has again reminded me that a new life in Jesus will give us eyes to see beyond the thrills of this earth and look forward to the new heaven and earth that God will reveal when Jesus appears once again.

If you have hung in there with me to this point, please take courage in the name of Jesus and don't be afraid of the things you may be going through at this moment or the things to come. Be careful not to seek the cheap thrills of this world to satisfy your immediate need to escape. Set your eyes only on Jesus, call out to Him.... and I promise... he will take time to meet with you, he will remind you of His story of forgiveness, healing, restoration and life.... and He will intercede on your behalf to the Father, just as my children...experienced.

If you haven't found your way into the family of God just yet, or have faded away [from His blessings by] chasing the treasures of this world....I want to humbly encourage you to choose Jesus today and become part of His church. If you are not sure how, reach out to me and I will walk with you [through the steps].

May God bless you richly today and give you peace.

Darren

Yes, the key to true treasure is Jesus. He is our Savior, healer, restorer of life, and interceder. He wants us to live life connected to Him so that we can remain anchored in hope, joy, and peace. He wants us to communicate this hope, joy, and peace with others by sharing our stories over a cup of coffee or a meal, by participating in life together. Be bold, be brave, and be obedient to tell your story of God's goodness to someone. He is our Rock, our **Solid Ground!**

Soil Sifting Summary

- The **solid ground** we stand on is not by nature holy. It is made holy by the divine presence of our Holy God.
- People should recognize you in malls and restaurants and want a touch from "Jesus."
- The life and joy that God offers through Jesus far exceeds the temporary thrill of man's attempt to satisfy through the escape of amusement.
- Set your eyes only on Jesus, call out to Him, and He will take time to meet with you. He will remind you of His story of forgiveness, healing, restoration and life.
- Jesus will intercede on your behalf to the Father.

Digging into God's Word

- Exodus 3:5-10
- Luke 6:19
- Ephesians 3:20-21
- Hebrews 12:2-3
- Romans 8:26-27

Extracting Truths and Treasures

Made in the USA
Lexington, KY
27 October 2019